IMPACT together

Biblical Mentoring Simplified

Elisa Pulliam

Life Coach and Mentor

DEDICATION

Titus 2:3-5
teach the older women
train the younger women

For this generation of young women desperately
longing for older women to speak truth, grace, love,
wisdom, and hope into their souls as they do life together.

And for this generation of older women
longing to live a life of impact by investing in the next generation.

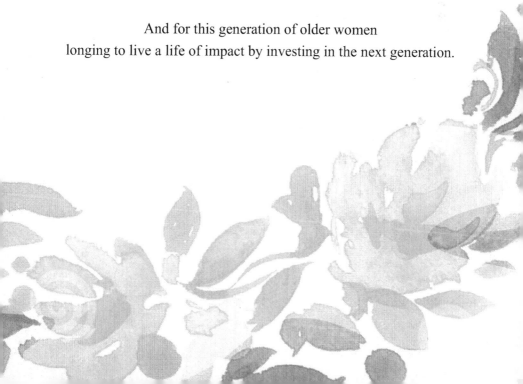

Table of Contents

INTRODUCTION

Mentoring Matters

As I listened beyond her words, I could tell the longing was real and deep. She wasn't making small talk in these last few moments of a busy conference weekend. Her confession was real and raw, as she admitted to me how grateful she would be if an older woman in her church would be willing to come alongside her as a mentor.

My heart fell hard. Again. That's because I've heard this longing before and been privy to the perspective of the one she's referring to—that older woman who seems to be forsaking a mentoring opportunity. But that is only one side of the story, as that older woman often feels she's not needed nor wanted ... that she's out of touch and the younger generation is simply too busy to slow down to spend time together.

Although conflicting schedules, work commitments, and family responsibilities are valid excuses for not being able to connect, the real issue is masked by excuses. Regardless of age, we women seem to have an insecurity streak that's a mile wide, keeping us from stepping beyond our comfort zones and reaching beyond the generational divide to connect at a heart-deep level.

Misconceptions, misunderstandings, and fears keep us from the blessing of mentoring relationships.

Until now.

Yes, now is the time to tackle every excuse and obstacle standing in your way! So will you join me in pursuing honest, hope-filled, life-changing mentoring relationships that are both Christ-centered and cross-generational? Regardless of your age, there is someone eager to impact your life as a biblical mentor, and I am certain that there is also someone awaiting your mentoring investment. I promise, this endeavor doesn't need to intimidate you. I've made the process simple, practical, and rooted in Scripture, as I've built upon the principles first published in a thirty-one day series at moretobe.com and later released in *Impact My Life: Biblical Mentoring Simplified* in 2012. This revised and expanded edition includes relevant information about the unique generational differences and valuable insights on how to cross the generational divide. It also takes a deeper look into Scripture, examining biblical characters and particular teachings that inspire a lifestyle of mentoring.

The blend of biblical principles, relevant illustrations, life coaching techniques, and creative ideas for simplifying mentoring will equip you to cultivate impactful, healthy, and God-honoring relationships with the women He has already placed in your life.

How to Use

Impact Together: Biblical Mentoring Simplified isn't about giving you more to do, but rather it's a prayerfully crafted tool designed to equip you to enjoy the fullness of mentoring relationships. Whether you are searching for a mentor or desire to become one, this book is written for you. *Impact Together* will enable you to discover your place in the body of Christ while uncovering the simple steps of cultivating Christ-centered mentoring relationships.

Impact Together: Biblical Mentoring Simplified divided into four key sections:

Part 1: Myths, Misconceptions, and Pure Motivations
Part 2: Eliminating Excuses
Part 3: The Six Steps of Mentoring
Part 4: Launch with Impact

Part 1 encourages you to understand the generational stereotypes and mentoring myths, while also pinpointing your motives in pursuing mentoring relationships. Part 2 considers the main excuses standing in the way of building healthy mentoring relationships. Part 3 details the action-steps of mentoring from a very practical perspective. Part 4 provides insight into how to mentor the tribe you feel called to impact today.

At the end of each chapter, you'll find Reflection Questions designed to help you grow in your faith and mature as a mentor. These questions are helpful for group discussion, as *Impact Together: Biblical Mentoring Simplified* is designed to be read with others. A leader's guide at the end provides format and suggestions to help you embrace such an opportunity with ease. The Impact Challenges spaced throughout the book provide opportunities for you to put the principles into action.

I pray for this journey to be marked by His love, filled with His grace, and infused with His hope as you uncover the work He is already doing in your life. May you catch the contagious vision of what it means to be purposefully connected with your sisters-in-Christ in every season and stage of life. Before you turn the page, pause and dedicate this journey to the Lord.

> *Oh Lord, open my eyes that I may see you already at work in my life. Prepare me to receive what You would have me learn. Lord, enable me to focus each time I sit down to read and reflect on the principles in this book. Father, may you give me insight so I will grow spiritually and emotionally as I dig into this material. Bring to the surface anything that is holding me back. Reveal to me Your truth, so I may embrace it and live it out with those you've called me to impact. In Jesus' name, Amen!*

PART ONE

Myths, Misconceptions, and Pure Motivation

*"We're not here for adoration or worship of God only, although that's number one.
If that were all we're for, God could take us straight to heaven, where our worship would be undistracted. No, the reason He leaves us here a while is so that we can make a mark on others before we go."*

Anne Ortlund

The Gentle Ways of a Beautiful Woman

1

Better Together

If you gave me only a few minutes to share my heart with you, one thing would quickly become apparently: I'm passionate about equipping women to experience life transformed for the sake of impacting the next generation. It's a both/and—my heart is split equally between investing in women and the ones they impact. That's because my life has been so dramatically shaped by the women who have taken time to invest in me, while I've had the privilege of speaking life into the lives of hundreds of teenage girls over the last twenty-plus years. I'm passionate about mentoring relationships because I've experienced the blessing both ways—the richness of having an older women pour into me, and the privilege of investing into the lives of those in the next generation. That's why I can testify that it's true when Scripture says "those who refresh others will themselves be refreshed" (Proverbs 11:25 NLT). When it comes to mentoring, it's equally true. It's not just about giving. It's also about receiving.

Mentoring is refreshing because it brings us together in a way God designed.

To be honest, I never set out to become a mentor or to advocate so strongly for it. This mission has been an overflow of the life God ordained for me, which included living at a boarding school with my husband and raising our children, immersed in a world of teenagers and a tight-knit community for eighteen years. It was natural for me to get advice from older women as much as it was to connect with the teenage girls crawling all over the place. I've discovered, however, that these organic relationships aren't limited to a boarding school environment. Living in normal suburbia has convinced me that mentoring relationships can be cultivated in churches, schools, work places, and even online communities.

As King Solomon writes in Ecclesiastes, there is nothing new under the sun. The next generation has the same issues we had at their age—and when I say "next" I mean YOUR next. If you're eighty, then "next" is everyone younger than you ... and yes, that's a lot of people to choose from. If you're twenty, well, then it's not quite as big of a group! Regardless, their struggles are likely the same ones we've had and may even still be dealing with:

- insecurities about worth and appearance and value
- wondering about identity and purpose
- longing for unconditional love
- struggling with the comparison trap
- worrying about not being enough and being too much
- fears about the future

Even if technology and social media makes the millennials' world so much harder, the solutions to the obstacles they face are the same. God is the same yesterday, today, and tomorrow.

God has the answers we are all looking for because His truth is timeless.

While the truth found in Scripture and the leading of the Holy Spirit are accessible to all of us by faith in Jesus Christ, it's often more compelling when it's conveyed by someone who takes the time to invest in our lives. Wouldn't you agree? That's why it's so important to cultivate Christ-centered and cross-generational relationships—we are the vessels of the truth. We are the legacy of faith builders and hope-carrying world changers. Becoming a mentor is about more than feeling good and carrying a special title. It's about investing in the furthering of the kingdom of God while engaging the hearts of His people to take their place in the body of Christ.

God's creatively limitless when it comes to how He wants to impact your life through mentoring.

Friend, I promise you the authentic mentoring relationships you crave are not only a good thing, they are a God thing. Maybe, however, your pursuit of mentoring feels more like a desperate search rather than simply a good idea. That's how I felt twenty-plus years ago, long before I knew what biblical mentoring looked like. See, I grew up in a dysfunctional family (much like every other American) with a shaky faith foundation. My high school and college years were marked by rebellion and searching for love in all the wrong places. I ended up in London during my junior year in college and wrestled through what I believed about God.

Through a number of divine appointments, I came to believe that Jesus Christ died on the cross for the forgiveness of my sins (Romans 10:9-10). In one moment of faith, my life turned in a new direction, as I radically decided that I wanted to live for Him alone. (You can read the play-by-play of this awesome story in *Meet the New You: A 21-Day Plan for Embracing Fresh Attitudes and Focused Habits for Real Life Change*.) But even after becoming a Christian, I didn't know how to start applying the principles found in Scripture to everyday life. The desire was there, but the knowledge was not. After graduating and getting married shortly before turning twenty-three, the pressure was on to figure it all out, so I turned to the women at church and in my community to glean their wisdom and learn from their example. Isn't this what biblical mentoring is all about?

God was gracious to surround me with women whose hearts were steadfast on Him. Without a formula or a title to our relationships, I found myself being mentored organically, as I took notice of their lives and sought out their advice for specific issues. Through watching them, I discovered how to have a God-centered marriage and how to walk in forgiveness after all I had experienced. I learned how to parent in grace and truth with a good dose of creativity and consistency. I was challenged to consider my priorities and make room for my calling.

These grey hairs (if I may use such an expression with the utmost respect) shaped my life in priceless ways. They were willing to be used right where they were, without giving into the insecurities that plague us all. And yet, I nearly missed their value because I was searching for significance through having one single mentor. I'll never forget how I was overcome by jealousy when I heard a woman speaking at a conference and she declared her role as a mentor in the life of another woman nearly my age. I wanted that proclamation, and yet in that moment, God impressed on my heart a life-changing truth about mentoring relationships:

**If we search for one single mentor,
we'll miss out on the circle of mentors
we've already been given.**

Your mentors may already be active in your life, and you've not yet noticed. And the same goes for those you ought to be mentoring. Maybe it's that woman sitting in the same pew at church who always takes the time to talk with you. Maybe she's your next-door neighbor or the younger gal in your Bible study group, who you feel a longing to reach out to. Maybe it's the long-distance friend you met at a conference, who periodically checks in with you and asks the tough questions. God may choose for all of them to be a part of an organic community of mentors. The truth is that God has given us many mentors, if only we'd look at it from His perspective. They may not announce their influence from a platform, but they are there, quietly, organically, and beautifully investing in our lives as we do the same for others.

The world might simply call these type of women Christian friends, but I call them biblical mentors because these relationships span the generations and are not dependent on being in the same season in life. Additionally, the older women in these mentoring relationships are committed to three key principles:

1. **Following Christ distinctly in their personal lives.**

2. **Offering counsel based on the wisdom found in the Word.**

3. **Providing encouragement and modeling biblical life application through doing life side by side together.**

So, imagine for a moment what it would look like if you began to see the circle of mentors God has already placed in your life. Who do you look up to for their faith in Christ? Who always has wise counsel for you? Who is doing life side by side with you? And how are you serving, maybe unknowingly, as an older mentor, influencing those just a few paces behind you?

So, let me ask you a tough question. Is it time for you to ...

Forget the title?
Forget the rules?
Forget the expectations?

How about focusing on the people God's already placed near you while looking for ways to both receive and give His love, hope, and truth in everyday, non-threatening, super simple ways?

Together Is Better

When I think about why biblical mentoring has become so important to me, I realize it has much to do with the setting and culture in which we live. Our lives are busy. Our opportunities to deeply connect are few. Our focus is distracted. Our marriages are broken and families divided. Our mommas are working hard. Our emotional wounds are deep. Our guilt is paralyzing.

It is so easy to remain always in motion, never seeing the need before us to speak into the lives of others, especially the next generation. But this is not how God intended for us to live. Consider, for a moment, how it must have been when women met at a well to draw water to nourish their families. Did they talk? Share? Connect? Were they being nourished through the sharing of life together? But where does that happen today?

With our cell phones beeping and carpools clamoring, we don't connect unless we purpose ourselves to do so.

As a work-at-home mom, I can easily go four or five days without seeing other women. Oh my, that's lonely! Bible study and church provide a place to connect, but only if I have margin space to linger for a conversation. Making time for relationships, whether they are peer friendships or mentoring focused, require some degree of intentionality because of the sacrifice of time.

It's easy to push off people in the pursuit of accomplishing tasks, but in the end we'll pay the price that comes with loneliness and isolation.

God designed for to be knit together, not only in our families, but beyond. Should we be surprised? God created His body to function as a whole under the headship Christ: "Just as our bodies have many parts and each part has a special function, so it is with Christ's body. We are many parts of one body, and we all belong to each other" (Romans 12:4-5 NLT).

It's inherent to God's design that we are better together.

Biblical mentoring provides a way to pass the baton of faith-lived-out from one generation to the next. It's about doing life side by side, imparting biblical application through relationships, and not just teaching the Word in a Bible study context (although that may be part of the process). We need these in-the-flesh mentors, even if miles separate us at times, to speak to the cries of our hearts, cheer us on, challenge us with grace and truth, and beckon us to be who God created us to become, regardless of how old or young we may be. Wouldn't you agree?

Mentoring is timeless, ageless, and stage-less because it's for all of us.

Our mentoring circle may include our daughters and nieces, neighbors and friends, co-leaders and team members, all who need more of Christ's hope, more of His truth, and more encouragement for living out the Scriptures day by day. In a world that quickly dismisses God's Word as truth, our biblical mentoring relationships are critical to convey the gospel.

When we step into the mentoring circle, we get to be Christ-with-skin-on to others while painting a three-dimensional picture of what it looks like to live as a disciple of Christ. It's not a perfect picture that we're expected to present, but one in which God is the artist painting beautiful strokes on the canvas of our lives.

It's God's work in us that becomes the foundation for biblical mentoring.

Isn't that a freeing concept? It's not about getting our lives all together so that we can mentor, but rather being willing to be a sojourner on the road of transformation together. I know the challenges we face as women to feel effective and instrumental in the lives of others. It is all too easy to focus on our weaknesses, while making a myriad of excuses that keep us from being used by God for His glory in the important relationships that abound in our lives. For those of us who were not raised with biblical truths and never experienced the benefits of mentoring, it is easy to believe we could never step into significant mentoring roles. However, I am here to challenge you to think differently about your purpose and potential as a biblical mentor so that you may feel called, qualified, and equipped by God for such a task!

God is more than eager to use an enthusiastic soul than a seemingly qualified one.

It is the willing spirit that matters, not life experience, a gifted personality, or a plastic-perfect life. Expertise and degree qualifications do not matter to hurting hearts, lost souls, or women hungry for love wrapped in truth. There are really only two qualifications for being a biblical mentor:

1.   Being committed to the Word as truth while seeking to live it out daily (2 Timothy 3:16-17).

2.   Being open to God's leading to impact the next generation (Titus 2:3-5).

Biblical mentoring is about being rooted in the Word in order to apply it to everyday life and being willing to do life together with others. It isn't so much about how you mentor, where you mentor, or who you mentor, but the motives behind why you mentor.

We are qualified to mentor biblically when we follow Christ distinctly.

Being a child of God, through faith in Jesus Christ, is our starting place for embracing biblical mentorship, as the Holy Spirit works within us as our guide and counselor.

John 14:26 (NLT)
*But when the Father sends the Advocate as my representative—
that is, the Holy Spirit—he will teach you everything and will
remind you of everything I have told you.*

As the Holy Spirit leads and guides us, we can walk humbly in step with Him as we reach out to serve as mentors. We don't need a world of knowledge. We don't need to be theologians. We simple need to be willing and eager to see God use us as His coworkers.

> 1 Corinthians 3:9 (NIV)
> *For we are co-workers in God's service ...*

It's as simple as coming alongside someone else to give from the overflow of what you have, as little or as much as it might be.

We simply need to know "one more thing" to teach that "one thing" to someone else.

When we learn a particular verse, we can turn to another person and teach that verse. It may be only one verse, but from there we go back to our Bibles and learn another verse, so that we can teach again and again. Wouldn't you agree that biblical mentoring is that simple, too, where the Scriptures are taught through a combination of relationship and study of Scripture? It's in these organic relationships that we find the answers to questions we often struggle with in various seasons and stages of life, like:

> *Am I ever going to be loved the way I want to be loved?*
> *Am I totally messing up my life?*
> *Am I going to find a husband?*
> *Am I screwing up my children or my marriage?*
> *Am I needed in this community?*
> *Am I outdated?*
> *Am I valuable beyond what I can do for others?*
> *Am I really able to forgive like that?*

Christ-centered mentoring relationships provide a safe place for answering these questions, as we learn how to practically live out our faith by doing life together. Yes, that can be messy at times. Yes, it will require the risk of getting hurt or feeling foolish, as all honest-to-goodness relationships do. But, as it is said, "It's better to have loved and lost than to never have loved at all." So, if you'll trust me to lead the way, let's dive deeper into this journey of discovering the beauty of biblical mentoring relationships.

Mentoring Motivations

As we begin to look more closely at what it means to be mentored and step out as a mentor, we have to pause to take a pulse on the motivations hidden within our hearts.

> Jeremiah 17:9 (NIV)
> *The heart is deceitful above all things and beyond cure. Who can understand it?*

Oh yes, the heart is deceitful, which means your motives may be out of whack and sabotaging your mentoring relationships! So before we go any further, take time to read through the statements below and consider which ones resonate with you. Be honest. Go there. It's time to 'fess up your heart to God and allow Him to change your thinking (Romans 12:2) and thereby adjust your expectations.

The Reasons Why I Want to Mentor

- I want to see people live according to God's Word, by the power of His strength, love, and grace.
- I desire to see God's purpose and potential realized in the

lives of other women.
- I want to see my children embrace godly principles and biblical priorities.
- I hope to invest in spiritual daughters by meeting their practical and spiritual growth needs.
- I am willing to teach the Word to those young in their faith.
- I want to share the lessons I've learned along my journey of motherhood with younger moms.
- I am eager to impact tween, teen, or twenty-something girls with Holy Spirit-appointed opportunities.
- I want to mentor others because of the overflowing work of Christ in my life!

The "Not So Good" Reasons Why I Want to Mentor

- I want to fix the problems I see in others.
- I want to protect others from getting hurting.
- I love being used by God to help others.
- I feel like I know the best way life should be lived and want to share that with others.
- I can't help my own children, but at least I can help someone else's.
- I need to do this in order to have purpose in my life.
- I have to spend my time doing something Christian, so why not mentor.

Friend, these reasons may have some element of good in them, but overall, each one reflects a self-serving motive and, to some degree, a savior complex. There is only one Jesus who died on the cross for our sins. He's the one who can fix problems, not us. And any desire we have for someone else to fill a hole in our hearts or an emptiness in our lives is simply making a false god and won't accomplish what we're after.

It's from an overflow of what God is doing in us—filling us, loving us, healing us—that gives us the ability to mentor others.

The Reasons I Want to Be Mentored

- I want to grow in my understanding of Scripture and how to live it out.
- I want to develop my faith to endure the storms of life and soak up the blessings with gratitude.
- I want to know how to love my husband (now or in the future) with a pure heart, respect, and sincere devotion.
- I want to know how to raise my children (now or in the future) according to godly principles and to love the Lord their God with all their heart, mind, and soul.
- I want to discover how to use my gifts and talents to serve God's kingdom purposes.
- I want to be held accountable for my lifestyle choices.
- I want to be encouraged and supported in a way that causes me to grow in my faith.

The "Not So Good" Reasons I Want to Be Mentored

- I want someone to show me the right way to solve this problem and help me through it.
- I desperately need to replace the mom I never had.
- I want help raising my children.
- I can't manage life all by myself anymore.
- I am lost without someone telling me what to do.

- I've been through such an awful time in my life that I just need someone who can be a light to me right now.
- I don't have enough faith on my own.

Sister, these are deep issues that need tender loving care. A mentor most certainly can relieve the burden you feel, but no woman on the planet can fill these needs. I urge you to head in the direction that can serve you best: First, go to God and lay this all before Him. He will not leave you nor forsake you in any way. And, I wholeheartedly encourage you to speak with your pastor for the next step or to reach out to a counselor for support. You can find a Christian counselor in your area at the Focus on the Family website under "help."

The Ways Mentoring Is Happening Already in My Life

- I am committed to attending a Bible study or small group in order to be under the leadership and influence of godly women.
- I strive to carve out margin space for impromptu conversations with older women after church, Bible study, and other gatherings.
- I look for opportunities to connect with other women, either one-on-one or in a group setting on a monthly basis to develop relationships.
- I embrace the accountably offered by wiser Christian women, whenever they are willing to speak into my life.
- I take time to connect with wiser women outside of my "real-life" circle, if they are willing to spend time on the phone with me or message me, even if it is through social media.
- I am teachable when it comes to heeding the wisdom of a godly, older sister-in-Christ, whether it's over lunch, coffee, or a quick conversation in the hallway at church.

- I am willing to be challenged to grow my understanding of the Word through books and studies written by Christian women (and men), as these authors share their faith, life experience, and understanding of the Word in a relevant way.
- I am submitted to the work and leading of the Holy Spirit, especially as I spend time with Jesus and in the Word on a regular basis.

When Mentoring Is NOT Happening

Friend, it may be true that mentoring is not happening in your life— and for good reason. Are you walking through a tough season? Are you homebound due to illness? Are you pressed in from all sides with work and home responsibilities? Are you caring for special-needs children? Aging parents? A sick family member? There are seasons in which we can't be stretched any further. However, I encourage you to seek the Lord for His perspective for where you are at today. Maybe there's even one way you can embrace mentoring in your life while pressing forward in the season you find yourself in.

Can you now see how mentoring happens organically? It's not nearly as complicated as we like to make it! While there are plenty of techniques and biblical principles to unpack, I encourage you to begin looking around to see where God is already at work, cultivating a circle of mentor relationships all around you.

Reflection Questions

1. Are you tempted to put off pursuing mentoring relationships

in fear of getting hurt? If so, what would motivate you to step beyond the fear? Who can you confide in for support and encouragement?

2. What mentors has God already placed in your life? How can you thank them today? If there are none, take time to talk to the Lord and ask Him to reveal His perspective.

3. Who have you been mentoring all along, but didn't even realize it? Who might God be calling you to mentor organically, without a program or unrealistic expectations?

Impact Challenge

Spend time in quiet prayer, asking Jesus to speak to you directly about your influence on others and, moreover, who you're being influenced by. Make sure you have a Bible on hand and, if you feel the prompting, take the time to read a particular verse or passage. Let the Word change your thinking and transform your living from the inside out.

2

Cross-Wired Relationships

Have you ever considered how we find our purpose when we are connected to those in the family of God? Think about how you feel when you've been able to serve a friend in need. Or the satisfaction that comes when you can guide a younger gal with the wisdom you've gained tromping uphill through the messy trials of life. While mentoring relationships scratch an itch to feel needed, that's not the end goal. Mentoring isn't meant to be about serving ourselves. Mentoring relationships have a far greater purpose revealed in the heart of Paul's teaching in Titus 2.

Titus 2:3-5 (NLT)
Similarly, teach the older women to live in a way that honors God. They must not slander others or be heavy drinkers. Instead, they should teach others what is good. These older women must train the younger women to love their husbands and their children, to live wisely and be pure, to work in their homes, to do good, and to be submissive to their husbands. Then they will not bring shame on the word of God.

Take a close look at the step-by-step instructions:

> *teaching how to live in a way that honors God*
> *teaching what is good*
> *training how to love one's husband and children*
> *training how to live wisely and purely*
> *training how to care for one's home*
> *training how to "do good"*
> *training how to submit to their husbands (see Eph. 5:21)*

It's quite a list, don't you think? But don't miss the last point.
then they will not bring shame on the Word of God. This Titus 2 passage leads us to a powerful principle: We cultivate a testimony about God through the example set by the way we live, and that example communicates His purposes to the next generation.

Our testimony is written in our day in, day out lives, because it is in doing life together that we carry the greatest level of influence.

I have to admit, I hate to think of my day in, day out life being my testimony because I'm so keenly aware of how I fall short to give glory to God. Do you have any idea how many times I stumble with my family? Even though the Lord has done a miraculous work on my heart, setting me free from a legacy of abuse and uprooting every bit of bitterness and unforgiveness from my heart, I can still be a hot mess. Yes, that means I am human. And sometimes hormonal. But that doesn't mean it's okay. Rather, it's likely the very reason Paul began his instruction warning about the temptations that women will face, knowing full well the ripple effect of sin. He brings to light the areas we are all susceptible to, while urging us to pursue good and pure ways of living.

Paul warns us against slander, maybe because the quickest way to malign the Word of God is with our mouths, don't you think? Especially when you're as quick-tongued as I am! But it's not only our words that present a problem in our testimony, it's also our addictions and propensity to sin. What else could we add to the list besides drinking too much wine? How about shopping, food, social media, pornography? Don't they offer us unhealthy ways to numb out and illicit a high? Wouldn't you agree that we ought to resist these temptations, whether it's the impulsive urge to buy or binge or ingest the impurities of this world?

Paul urges us to put off our sin while putting on what is good and pure. While the pursuit of "good" may be obvious, our flesh-driven, comfort-craving nature is tempted to rebel. Think about it: Do we really want the older women in our lives, like our moms and mothers-in-law, telling us what to do? Sure, we want their love and support, but not their training. We want to figure it out on our own, doing it our way, just like we were when we were two years old. Aha, so maybe that's why mentoring becomes a challenge!

We've got to come to the table teachable and trainable.

It seems our teachers and trainers need to be a little more determined, especially in the face of opposition and distractions. Our independent nature is going to make it tough for them to mentor us, don't you think? So maybe that's why Paul sets forth such a call in this passage. He knows we'll run from it in every direction, but that doesn't keep him from tackling the tough stuff. He's as concerned with our self-care (or soul care) as he is with our relationships along with stewarding resources. For example, we might be offended by the instruction to be "busy at home," but what if we thought of it as stewardship of our space? It's not about the size or style of our dwellings. It's not about making an idol out of housekeeping or mastering the art of interior decorating, but rather it's about caring for our homes in a way that honors God. Isn't that a good idea?

We might also be miffed at Paul for urging wives to be submissive to their husbands. Is this a point of contention for you? It was for me early on in my faith, as I thought submissive meant I had no say and would be bossed around. I had no idea that submission in a marriage could be such a blessing, because it's not about oppressive leadership, rather it's about following in Christ's example. Paul is not suggesting that females are second-class citizens to be ruled and managed. He's reminding us of the stinking apple-eating-incident, when the order of things went awry. God declared from that point on a woman would desire to rule over her husband (Genesis 3:16). However, in Christ, that desire can be transformed by the power of the Holy Spirit, as she yields to her husband as unto Christ and he does the same.

Ephesians 5:21
Submit to one another out of reverence for Christ.

We can choose to honor God, or utterly rebel against Him, when it comes to our relationships, resources, and how we live our personal lives. We get to choose, and yet our choices will reap a consequence or a blessing, not only for us but for others. Isn't that a sobering thought?

It's never just about you or me. It's about the generation that is learning from our example.

That's what I think Paul was getting at in this passage. He's concerned with the bigger picture while urging us to take up our position in the body of Christ. He's seeing our impact as women, one to another, older to younger, mother to daughter, aunt to niece. It is in these organic relationships that we get to mentor in "cross-wired" relationships tied together through the normal routines that ebb and flow throughout our days.

Cross-Wired Together

What do I mean by "cross-wired" relationships? Imagine, for a moment, the inner workings of an electrical cord, where there are three individual wires working together for one purpose. From the outside it looks like one cord, but really there are three individual components—one hot, one neutral, and one is considered the ground wire, wrapped in its own casing and intertwined together into an outer casing. This is exactly what I imagine when I think of the generations being wired together—individuals with their own distinct purpose and place, but coming together as one body of Christ and for the glory of God. Can you imagine anything more purposeful or beautiful?

Cross-wired relationships forged in light of the Titus 2 passage fulfill three key principles of biblical mentoring:

1. **Discipling** – teaching biblical truths in everyday life and, at times, through intentional Bible study.

2. **Modeling** – modeling biblical principles in everyday life together.

3. **Connecting** – spending time together doing everyday things.

Can you imagine what it might be like to pursue relationships with a diverse group of women in various stages and seasons of life with this focus on discipling, modeling, and connecting based on your own personal and growing relationship with Christ? It's this type of intentionality in Christ-centered mentoring relationships that makes them slightly different from peer friendships—although they can be one in the same. One of my most beloved mentors was only a year older than me, yet she was able to speak truth and wisdom into my life because she grew up knowing the Lord. She was both my friend and my mentor, because she discipled me, modeled a godly life for me, and connected with me on a regular basis. Can you think of a friend, maybe close to your own age, who has served you as a biblical mentor? Or can you think of someone who is older than you and has impacted your life through discipleship as well as modeling a godly example and taking time to connect with you? Maybe you didn't call her a mentor, and yet, that's exactly a taste of what you've experienced.

Discipleship Plus Biblical Mentoring

As we think about the ins and outs of biblical mentoring, we get our cues from Jesus first and foremost. Consider the way He came alongside the disciples, modeled His Father's instructions in action, answered their questions, responded to their needs, and challenged them forward in their calling to glorify God. Isn't this biblical mentorship in the way we're defining it?

**Jesus was both their friend and their teacher.
A mentor and a man who discipled others.**

Jesus set a pattern for us to follow as we answer the call to mentor by first being a disciple of Christ and then going forward as He leads us to those we're called to disciple.

Matthew 28:19
Therefore go and make disciples of all nations, baptizing them in the name of the Father and of the Son and of the Holy Spirit.

The broad definition of "disciple" means to be a student of a particular teacher and follower of their doctrine. Christian discipleship is clearly focused on Jesus and the Scriptures as the foundation of doctrine. Traditionally, mentoring, in contrast, refers to what takes place in a workplace or in an academic environment, where a seasoned employee or older student comes alongside a younger cohort to train, guide, and encourage in a particular area of expertise. Biblical mentoring, however, combines the heart of discipleship and methods of mentoring to cultivate relationships steeped in truth through living out Scripture application side by side.

In a biblical mentoring relationship, the goal is to train the younger person or believer in every area of life, not only through teaching but also by example, incorporating God and His Word into every teachable moment. This principle is laid out in Deuteronomy 6:5-7, which conveys how to live a life that teaches by example, particularly with one's children, but certainly not limited to that relationship.

Deuteronomy 6:5-7
And you must love the Lord your God with all your heart, all your soul, and all your strength. And you must commit yourselves wholeheartedly to these commands that I am giving you today. Repeat them again and again to your children. Talk about them when you are at home and when you are on the road, when you are going to bed and when you are getting up.

As we think about the role of biblical mentoring in our lives, it's easy to see how this passage describes the way a mom can mentor her children right at home. However, in a world marred by divorce and death, children who need mothers and fathers abound. There are an endless number of motherless young people (and young is always relative) desperately needing the practical gift of time, love, and personal investment. Stepping into the gap, with Deuteronomy 6 as syllabus, is a beautiful way to serve as a biblical mentor. It looks something like this:

Principles for Biblical Mentoring

- A biblical mentor embraces an active, personal relationship with Jesus Christ, believing that He died on the cross for the forgiveness of her sins (Romans 10:9-10).

- A biblical mentor seeks to learn the Word, apply it to life, and follow the leading of the Holy Spirit (Hebrews 4:12; 2 Timothy 3:16).

- A biblical mentor demonstrates an active commitment to the body of Christ by attending church, serving using her gifts and talents, and willingly coming under the authority of a pastor and leadership body (Romans 12).

If you can agree to each of these statements, you are already living as a disciple of Christ, and the overflow of your relationship with Him will purposefully influence others as you lead, teach, model, and encourage those you mentor. However, if you're not sure if this describes your relationship with God or faith walk, I would recommend flipping to the end of this book to read the chapter on Becoming a Disciple of Christ.

Reflection Questions

1. What parts of Titus 2 resonate with you, and why? Which parts of Paul's instruction cause you frustration, and why?

2. What do you think of the "Principles for Biblical Mentoring" statements? Which ones resonate with you? Which don't, and why?

3. If discipleship is about growing in your understanding of Scripture and mentoring is about learning the truths through a relationship, can you think of areas of your Christian walk you would like to grow in and seek mentorship?

Impact Challenge

Take the time to look up Titus 2:3-5 in multiple translations and consider the many different ways women are called to engage with and impact the next generation. Then rewrite the passage as a personal prayer as you yield to God your desire for mentorship to be a part of your life.

3

Bridging The Gap

There's only one reason I enjoy going to a doctor's office and it has nothing at all to do with my health. For the last decade or so, when the nurse looks over my chart, looks at my age, and sees how many children I've had, I get to hear the sweetest of words: "Wow, you don't look that old!" I can't help but laugh out loud. First off, it's only four children. Second off, it's likely due to the oil-producing glands of my Italian bloodline—the same bloodline that gave me the worst case of acne anyone ever laid eyes on and was one of the many reasons I hated my teenage years.

While I'm slightly grateful my oily skin has led to fewer wrinkles, I'm pretty sure that's not the only thing contributing to my "youth-fulness." I actually believe it has more to do with my experience living at a boarding school for nearly two decades. Spending the first twenty years of adulthood living with teenagers will either keep you young or make you age faster.

Being immersed with the next generation has deeply shaped my sensitivity to how each generation has its own nuances of thinking and thereby living. Combine that experience with being the daughter of Baby Boomers and highly influenced by my Traditionalist generation mother-in-law while raising my own Gen Zers (also known as Millennials), and well, I'm a generational hodgepodge passionate about making sense of our differences. Maybe you're wondering, "So what? Just accept it and move on?" Or maybe you're not even sure what I just said because referring to the generations is like speaking another language. Yes, it's jargon, but it's worth unpacking because understanding the impact of generational mindsets is key to bridging the gap between the generations. Before I give you the play by play, how about taking a little quiz to see what you know about the generations? See if you can match the decade to their description.

Generations

Traditionalists/Veterans (1900-1945)
Baby Boomers (1946-1964)
Gen X (1965-1980)
Gen Y/Millenials (1981–2000)

Character Descriptions

Generation _____
Self-reliance
Crave structure
Skeptical
Independent thinker

Generation _____
Respect authority
Self-sacrifice
Duty
Family

Generation _____
Multitasking
Tenacity
Entrepreneurial
Tolerant

Generation _____
Workaholics
Quality
Personal fulfillment
Financial rewards

Okay, now that I've brought you back to high school with a surprise quiz, I promise your grade doesn't count for anything. I'm not going to give you the answer just yet, as I want you to see it all in context so you can use this information to develop rich relationships with the women God has put in your life.

Understanding Our Differences

Have you ever considered how each generation stands apart from one another based not only on their age but their unique experiences? Think about it for a moment. What major political, social, or pop-culture movement has impacted your life? What experience do you share with those in your peer group that in a moment, you can be caught up in recounting the "when, where, and how" of an event? Was it the day JFK was shot? Or when the Challenger crashed? Do you remember OJ Simpson's highway chase? Or seeing the news report as 9/11 was unfolding? These events, traumatic as they may be, shaped your life and bond you with those who experienced it at your age.

Maybe it's not so much a national event that depicts your generational experience but rather the social norms and entertainment that marked your early adulthood. Do you remember the first rotary phone or first portable phone? How about a black-and-white television compared to a flat screen TV? What about when gas was less than a $1 a gallon and milk was no more than $2? The world around us is ever-changing, along with social norms, technology, and life-altering events.

We can't help but be shaped by our life experiences as well as the influence of the generation that comes before us.

Our parents, teachers, coaches, and pastors all speak their values into our lives, which have been shaped by their experience. Understanding these values, which are a by-product of our experiences, can lead to healthier relationships and opportunities for connecting, not only in mentoring relationships but also within our families, work places, and church communities.

We feel what we feel, value what we value, and believe what we believe, because of what we've experienced and been taught.

So what would it look like to really understand the perspective we each come from? Imagine how that simple step may be a bridge builder toward deeper relationships. Take some time to peer through the lens of time to see how experiences have shaped the values and the style of each generation.

The Generational Differences[1]

TRADITIONALISTS

Alternate Names	Silent
	Veterans
	GI Generation

1 Sources: http://davetgc.com/Generational_Differences.html; http://teaching-millenials.pbworks.com/w/page/19887051/Generational%20Differences; http://www.people-results.com/communication-ages/generational-differences/; http://www.wmfc.org/uploads/GenerationalDifferencesChart.pdf http://opi.mt.gov/pub/rti/EssentialComponents/Leadership/Present/Understanding%20Generational%20Differences.pdf; https://managementisajourney.com/fascinating-numbers-15-influential-events-that-shaped-generation-x/; http://www.pewsocialtrends.org/2015/03/19/comparing-millennials-to-other-generations/; http://www.marketingteacher.com/the-six-living-generations-in-america/; https://www.quora.com/What-was-the-most-popular-music-for-each-decade-1900-1909-1910-1919-etc; https://en.wikipedia.org/wiki/List_of_the_longest-running_Broadway_shows

Dates	1900-1945
Experiences	World War I
	World War II
	Great Depression
	Pre-Feminism
	Oklahoma! (Broadway)
	Big Band Music
	Bing Crosby
Values	Respect Authority
	Self-Sacrifice
	Duty
	Hard Work
	No need for feedback
	Family
	Community involvement
Dislikes	Waste
	Technology
Message	Experience is respected.
	No news is good news.
	Marriage is for life.
Communication	Formal
	Memo
	One-to-One
	Conversations
	Face-to-face

BABY BOOMERS

Alternate Names	Me Gen
Dates	1946-1964
Experiences	Vietnam
	Space Exploration
	Atomic Age
	Rock and Roll
	'60 -'70s Hippies
	First TV
	First divorce
	My Fair Lady (Broadway)
	Hello Dolly (Broadway)
	South Pacific (Broadway)
	The King and I ((Broadway)
	Doo-Wop
	R&B
	Beatles
Values	Workaholics
	Efficiency
	Quality
	Personal fulfillment
	Doesn't want feedback
	Titles
	Financial rewards
	"Can-do" attitude
	Optimism
Dislikes	Laziness

	Too much tech
Message	Work to live.
	You are valued and needed.
Communication	In person
	Teamwork
	Meetings

GEN X

Alternate Names	Latchkey Kids
	MTV Gen
Dates	1965-1980
Experiences	Desert Storm
	Cold War
	Fall of Berlin Wall
	AIDS
	Mass media
	Personal computers
	Latchkey kids
	'70 -'80s Yuppies
	Single parents
	Feminism
	A Chorus Line (Broadway)
	Cats (Broadway)
	Annie (Broadway)
	Simon & Garfunkel
	Rolling Stones
	Grateful Dead Band

Values	Self-reliance
	Crave structure
	Skeptical
	Independent thinker
	Asks for feedback
	Work-life balance
Dislikes	Red tape
	Hype
	Labels
	Brand names
Message	Do it your way and forget the rules.
	Freedom is the best reward.
Communication	Direct
	Immediate

GEN Y

Alternate Names	First Digitals
	Echo Boom
	Millennial
	Mosaics
Dates	1981-2000
Experiences	Persian Gulf War
	Internet
	Cloning
	School shootings

College is for everyone
Video games
Phantom of the Opera (Broadway)
Les Miserables (Broadway)
Annie Get Your Gun (Broadway)
Madonna
Michael Jackson

Values   Multitasking
Tenacity
Schedule everything
Academic pressure
Tolerant
Goal orientated
Frequent feedback
Social justice
Technology

Dislikes   Negativity
Slowness

Messages   You will work with other bright people.
Meaningful work is rewarding.
Do not live to work.

Communication   Email
Voicemail
Texting

GEN Z

Alternate Names	Gen Z
	iGeneration
	Millennial
Dates	2001-Present
Experiences	War on terror
	9/11
	ISIS
	Credit market collapse
	Cell phones
	Record number of births in 2006, which outnumbered the Baby Boomers
	Hairspray (Broadway)
	Kinky Boots (Broadway)
	Newsies (Broadway)
	Hamilton (Broadway)
	Kelly Clarkson
	Justin Bieber
	Taylor Swift
Values	Oversaturated with brands
	KYOG – kids growing older younger
	Savvy consumers
Dislikes	To be determined
Messages	To be determined
Communication	Texting and Social Messaging

The Broken Bridge Issue

Can you see how the generations have been influenced by cultural, political, and overall life experiences? Do those strange values and polarizing statements you've heard from your parents' generation make more sense now? Is your frustration with the younger generation more founded? Can you see why you think the way you do about certain topics?

Our values and styles of communication are so engrained in the culture we've been raised in and by those of influence over us, and these beliefs play out in our pursuit of cross-wired mentoring. Let me give you an example to help you connect the dots. We celebrated my mother-in-law's eighty-fifth birthday with a simple, family-focused dinner at home. It was exactly her speed to be surrounded by her loved ones. As we were approaching the table, Nana, as we call her, happened to have her iPhone in hand. Oh yes, she looks like a digital native, but really hates the thing. We all like to give her a hard time, in a respectful way, about her love-hate … or really hate … relationship with technology, so I seized the opportunity: "Mom, you know we're not supposed to have phones at the table." She responded with, "Well, I'm not on the phone. I'm checking my email." We all chuckled as I pushed back, "Okay, no screens at the table then."

As we grabbed hands to pray, she interrupted by saying how much she sincerely hates the stupid phone. She can't hear on it. She can't be heard on it. And she doesn't want to use it at all. And that's why she's told Jesus she's had enough with the phone and is more than ready to go be with Him, to which we all reacted with firm opposition. Oh yeah, over the frustration of using a stupid little piece of technology, she's ready to skip out of this world and leave the rest of us tethered to our screens.

Wouldn't you agree that my mother-in-law's response is all too common among the Traditionalists, but not only when it comes to cell phones? I've seen it play out in other ways, too. Only a week prior to Nana's birthday, the conference board I was a part of received a hand-written note from the sweetest woman frustrated that she never received any information about the upcoming event, apart from a postcard with a web address for more information. She included a self-addressed stamped envelope and a request for a phone call in order to purchase tickets. Bless her heart, our choice to move toward web-based promotions in order to save a few dollars caused her to feel out of the loop. We never meant to overlook a group of women we desperately want to be a part of our community, for they bring to the table wisdom and perspective the rest of us don't yet have.

It's not only the Traditionalists who feel out of touch and overlooked. I have a friend who recounted a story of a Baby Boomer confessing her frustration with connecting with her daughter-in-law because the daughter-in-law prefers to text while she prefers to call. She was adamant that she would not learn how to text when her daughter-in-law could just pick up the phone. Is this a matter of stubborn pride? Fear of looking stupid? Insecurity? What causes any of us to resist learning a new thing? Regardless, something about texting made her dig in her heels even though it was costing her connection with her daughter-in-law, until one of the other Gen Xers in the Bible study group showed her how to record a message and send it via text. Voila, a solution for the moment.

Yes, I do believe technology is a serious obstacle in wiring the generations together. But it's not the tech that's the problem—it's the values that are associated with technology that we have to consider. For example, the Baby Boomers value independence, efficiency, and in-person interactions. For this generation, computers and cellphones work against those values instead of being a tool to meet the need. Think about it practically: In order to have a women's gathering at church, you have to find out about it online, register at a website, plunk down your credit card info into the cyber world, and show up for a multi-media presentation. For Traditionalists and Baby Boomers, it's overcomplicated and overwhelming. Yet for the Gen X, Y, and Zers, whose lives have been built around technology, it's normal and necessary.

On the one hand, "So what!" Isn't that the mindset in the face of this obstacle? Doesn't the culture perpetuate the belief that each generation will have a new tool to play with and the old-timers need to either figure it out or fade away? Is the saying, "Well, you can't teach an old dog new tricks?" really the answer? As Christians, shouldn't we be seeking a way to connect and include rather than dismissing the older generation so callously?

If we don't find a way to cross the tech and cultural divide, our ministries and churches will lose the involvement of the wisest among us.

Have you noticed how women in their late 50s and older are stepping down from leadership teams and not stepping into roles where they could plan events, lead studies, and engage in ministries? These gray-haired women have lived long enough to discern what is godly, "Grey hair is a crown of glory; it is gained by living a godly life" (Proverbs 16:31 NLT).

So why are the 40-somethings, who are balancing full-plates of motherhood and work, strapped with leadership responsibilities? Because the way ministries function in this day and age makes the older gals feel out of touch and overwhelmed. They slink back and hope they'll find a place to contribute within their comfort zone ...

or maybe not at all. And the by-product is that a young generation of women feels lost and alone without godly, older mentors.

We need to look at our generational differences and debunk the myths while finding solutions for the real issues that need our attention.

"Clearly people of different age groups see the world in different ways and bring different experiences and skills to the table. Lassoing those skills to get that bronco moving forward with all of its energy intact is the goal. It's like any other relationship issue: If you ignore it, the relationship will fail. As research scientist Jennifer Deal notes, 'The so-called generation gap is, in large part, the result of miscommunication and misunderstanding, fuelled by common insecurities and the desire for clout.'" [2]

Wouldn't you say this is a gap worth closing? Let's find a solution for how to crosswire the generations together and foster a culture of embracing biblical mentoring relationships.

Reflection Questions

1. As you consider the descriptions about each of the different types of generations, what stands out to you? What was interesting? Surprising? Visible in others?

2. What are some of the stereotypes you've had about the different generations before reading this chapter?

---

2 Source: http://www.theglobeandmail.com/report-on-business/careers/career-advice/top-12-workplace-myths-misunderstood-by-all-generations/article559081/?page=all

3. How have those stereotypes been an obstacle in connecting with others?

Impact Challenge

Take time to think about the people who are a part of your everyday life and ask God to reveal to you the ways you may have expressed criticism toward or been frustrated with them from time to time as a result of generational differences.

- Do you think you need to seek God's forgiveness for the attitude in your heart and maybe even your words?

- Who do you need to reach out and apologize to?

- How can you strive to be a connector rather than a divider in your relationships as you think about these generational differences?

4

Debunking the Generational Myths

As we dive into the myths that make mentoring a challenge, I'd love to encourage you to stop and think about the stereotypes you've inherited or have adopted as your own.

What goes through your mind when you see a pack of teenagers at the mall?

What thoughts race through your head when you pass an old lady driving too slowly in the left-hand lane?

How have you conveyed some of your age-based stereotypes onto the next generation?

How have your opinions about "the way things should be done" polarized your relationships with others?

Oh yes, the generational myths are perpetuated by you and me. We unknowingly believe myths, and often lies, and pass them on to the next generation. As I share about in *Meet the New You*, this is the very reason we need to pursue a *Trap and Transform* lifestyle—by trapping our thoughts and making them obedient to Christ, and seeking to be transformed by the renewing of our minds according to the truth of Scripture (1 Corinthians 10:5; Romans 12:2). It's a daily discipline worthy of putting into action as we seek to cultivate mentoring relationships, and it is certainly a process that sets the foundation for debunking the generational myths and finding solutions for bridging the gap together.

Myth 1: They are too out of touch.

It's so interesting how this myth about being out of touch is used by the younger generation as well as the older generation. How could it be true of a 30-something and 60-something? Well that's because for a 30-something, there's a 20-something who seems to know more. For a 40-something, there's a 30-something, and so on. It's the "someone forgot to send me the memo" syndrome that plagues all of us in this information-overloaded world.

There's always something we won't know. The truth is that the older generation will at times feel out of touch as culture and technology change at a rapid speed. As a result, it becomes the responsibility of both generations to reach toward each other, seeking to learn and grow together in a reverse mentoring approach. According to a Barna study describing how to connect with Millenials in a church context, "reverse mentoring has come to describe the kind of give and take between young and experienced leaders. Effective ministry to Millennials means helping these young believers discover their own mission in the world, not merely asking them to wait their turn."[3]

I wonder, however, is reverse mentoring a new concept or just a new label? If we look to Scripture, we see the pattern for serving each other spelled out in Romans 12:4-5 and more thoroughly in 1 Corinthians 12:

> 1 Corinthians 12:18-22 (NLT)
> *But our bodies have many parts, and God has put each part just where he wants it. How strange a body would be if it had only one part! Yes, there are many parts, but only one body. The eye can never say to the hand, "I don't need you." The head can't say to the feet, "I don't need you." In fact, some parts of the body that seem weakest and least important are actually the most necessary. And the parts we regard as less honorable are those we clothe with the greatest care. So we carefully protect those parts that should not be seen, while the more honorable parts do not require this special care. So God has put the body together such that extra honor and care are given to those parts that have less dignity. This makes for harmony among the members, so that all the members care for each other. If one part suffers, all the parts suffer with it, and if one part is honored, all the parts are glad.*

We often consider this passage in light of skill and gifting, but isn't age diversity as much a part of this need as well? Wisdom is a gift that comes from God and also through life experience, which the younger generation needs to receive. Yet, some skill comes through training and exposure that the older generation might not get in their season and stage in life. What does it look like for the older to reach out with their "lack of" and receive from the younger, as the younger

---

3 Source: https://www.barna.org/barna-update/millennials/682-5-ways-to-connect-with-millennials#.VvA2hBIrLdc

reaches to the older for what they're missing too? Could that be another way to strive toward completeness in the body of Christ?

Myth 2: They can't live without their screens and aren't interested in real life relationships.

Oh yes, the actions of the Gen X, Y, and Zers make this one a hard myth to refute, since actions speak louder than words. But the truth is, our screens (yes, I lump myself into this category) have become to us what rotary phones, microwaves, and VCRs were to our parents and grandparents. We see them as commonplace because they are such an integrated part of our lives. We use our computers and smart phones for work, ministry, pleasure, connection, and organization. So, yes, we can't live without our screens the way we're accustomed to doing so in the same way frozen dinners and fast food were tools for those who lived before current technology.

Being tech-tethered doesn't mean the younger generation isn't interested in having "real life" relationships. On the contrary! Screenbased interactions pale in comparison to "real life" relationships. A friend one hundred miles away may love deeply, but she can't sit with you in the emergency room. Yes, a Facebook account flooding with prayers comforts the soul, but it doesn't replace a friend holding your hand. A casserole delivered in a time of grief with a real, live hug is a valuable gift—it's the hug that's priceless.

So my challenge for all of us is this: Can we look past the screens to see what's going on beneath the surface? How can we practically embrace our place in the family of God as His chosen, holy, and dearly loved children, and extend compassion, kindness, humility, gentleness, and patience toward each other?

> Colossians 3:12 (NIV)
> *Therefore, as God's chosen people, holy and dearly loved, clothe yourselves with compassion, kindness, humility, gentleness, and patience.*

Yes, the digital natives among us might need to put their screens down. And the Baby Boomers and Traditionalists may need to guard against criticism, remembering the new-fangled gadgets their own mommas once thought were unnecessary. Ah, yes, there will always be a new distraction that seems to overcomplicate life. But what is unnecessary to one may be normal to another, so how about we pursue kindness over critique?

Myth 3: They are judging me.

Wouldn't you agree that the feeling of being judged is an issue for every one of us? Is it any surprise that the younger generation feels like everything they do is under the critical eye of the older generation? How often do they hear well-meaning comments, criticism, and constructive critique? Although Gen X, Y, and Zers crave feedback, they want to solicit it on their own terms. If they are in a teachable mindset, then the feedback is helpful instead of coming across as judgmental.

The older generation experiences a sense of being judged too, but from a different perspective. When their advice is not heeded, they can't help but feel rejected. They also fear being judged when they don't know how to keep up with the changing times or refuse to participate in a certain kind of activity.

This sense of being judged breaks down relationships. So what's the solution? How about if we battled our tendency to feel judged by turning to the truth found in the Word? If the Scriptures are able to judge the thoughts and attitudes of the heart, then shouldn't we seek God and His Word to be the judge of our actions and beliefs?

> Hebrews 4:12 (NIV)
> *For the word of God is alive and active. Sharper than any double-edged sword, it penetrates even to dividing soul and spirit, joints and marrow; it judges the thoughts and attitudes of the heart.*

How often are we more concerned by what others will think of us rather than pleasing God alone (Galatians 1:10)? Maybe if we shifted our attention and asked God to reveal to us the truth, we may be less offended and even more teachable. Sometimes, the wisdom we need may come through criticism. Likewise, the challenge to get out of our comfort zone may feel frightening. Both, however, can be used by God to accomplish His purposes in us and for those around us, too.

Myth 4: They don't want to learn from me.

At first glance, you might think this myth is about how the older generation feels, yet it actually goes both ways. Yes, a Traditionlist might feel too outdated to have a heart-to-heart conversation with a Gen Zer. However, a Gen Yer gifted with a teaching ability may feel like it's wrong for her to speak at the ladies tea, considering the wisdom of the older women attending. Wouldn't Paul counter both arguments, reminding us to use the gifts God's given us (1 Corinthians 12), regardless of age:

1 Timothy 4:11-14 (MSG)
Get the word out. Teach all these things. And don't let anyone put you down because you're young. Teach believers with your life: by word, by demeanor, by love, by faith, by integrity. Stay at your post reading Scripture, giving counsel, teaching. And that special gift of ministry you were given when the leaders of the church laid hands on you and prayed—keep that dusted off and in use

The truth is we all have something of value that's worth imparting on someone else, regardless of age. Yes, years and wisdom often go hand in hand, but the body of Christ is encouraged to use their gifts all the time and as God leads.

Philippians 1:6 (NIV)
... being confident of this, that he who began a good work in you will carry it on to completion until the day of Christ Jesus.

God will no doubt wire us together in the most unexpected of ways, because His plan is to work through us throughout our lives.

Myth 5: They are self-absorbed.

Is this generation of Gen X, Y, and Zers really self-absorbed? Well, by the looks of it, maybe. We have the whole "i" generation of technology, but does that mean it's all about me, myself, and I? We have selfie-camera capabilities and selfie-sticks in order to capture our "selves" for the world to see on our social media feeds. Forget having our name in lights, it's all about the likes. The more the better, even if people we don't know nor will ever meet adore our viral photo! Like my daughter's acquaintance from school posting her prom proposal picture on Twitter and tagging the artist of the song that the guy used to pop the question. Well, Mr. Rap Star happened to notice the tweet and re-tweeted to his followers. Within twenty-four hours this girl had over eight thousand likes on her picture. Ooohhh, you could imagine the teen chatter over being so insanely noticed! I couldn't help but wonder, "And so what?" Yet, there's this thing about being seen, even if it's only virtually and by strangers, that makes each of us swell on the inside even if we won't confess to it on the outside. But does that behavior make us self-absorbed or does it simply reflect a deep need to be seen? And is that need magnified more than ever in our fast-pasted, information-overloaded, families-divided world? Yes, we have to consider that the by-product of a fifty percent divorce rate could end up with children clamoring for attention—even adult children.

Is what appears to be self-absorption nothing more than a cry for unconditional and undistracted love?

Ah, maybe. And yet, we've got to pause to consider how the Traditionalists process this need. They are the generation who sacrificed their lives for their country in WWI and WWII, never thinking about themselves but willing to give up self for the sake of others. Maybe the Baby Boomers were the first generation who really started focusing more on self than others, but that's because of the pain they endured, reeling from the trauma of the Vietnam and Korean wars, and then experiencing the consequences of their own sexual revolution?

It appears that self-absorption began long before selfies became commonplace, and at the heart of it were wounds deeply hidden by a wildly independent, non-conformist streak.[4] We might want to blame the culture and politics, but self-absorption is really selfishness in disguise, and it's been a part of our human nature since the beginning of time:

> Philippians 2:3 (NLT)
> *Don't be selfish; don't try to impress others. Be humble, thinking of others as better than yourselves.*

Our flesh will forever be consumed with self in the endless pursuit of defining our worth. Our selfish behavior is nothing but a cry for significance. If that's the case, then why not become a people who answer this cry for each other?

Imagine seeing the selfishness in each other and reaching toward it with practical signs of love—maybe a note, an offer to pray, or taking the initiative to grab a cup of coffee together. Come to think of it, maybe self-absorption should be like a red flag for pinpointing which relationships to pursue for cross-centering mentoring. Could it be that those who display the most selfishness are the ones who need the most Christ-centered love?

Myth 6: They are too busy for me.

I'm warning you, before I start in on this myth that this one is a hot-button for me. If I could count the number of times I've been criti-

---

4 Sources: http://www.thegenxfiles.com/2009/06/10/7-myths-about-generation-x/; http://www.theglobeandmail.com/report-on-business/careers/career-advice/top-12-workplace-myths-misunderstood-by-all-generations/article5590081/?page=all; https://www.barna.org/barna-update/millennials/687-millennials-and-the-bible-3-surprising-insights#.VvA2fBIrLdc

cized by an older woman for being too busy, I'd be rich enough that I could stop working all together. Yet, I know that those words spoken at the worst of times often came from a place of love and concern. These precious older women were concerned for the ramifications on my health, my family, and maybe even my spiritual life. And yet rather than offering to help in practical ways, they wanted me to change my ways—ways I couldn't always change.

Wouldn't you agree that we're not just busy for busy sake? The reality is that the fullness of our plates has to do with our God-given wiring (something we'll talk about in part 2) as well as the social and economic pressures upon us in this day and age. We're busy because we have the opportunity to pursue hobbies and activities and ministries and jobs that bring us joy. We're busy because we don't want our children to miss out on experiences—maybe because they were so significant to us and maybe because we never got to take advantage of such opportunities. We're busy because we don't know how to say no nor how to break free of the hamster wheel of social pressure. We're busy because we don't know how to keep a Sabbath, even though it's as equally important to God as not killing nor stealing or committing adultery.

Exodus 20:8-15 NIV
"Remember to observe the Sabbath day by keeping it holy. You have six days each week for your ordinary work, but the seventh day is a Sabbath day of rest dedicated to the LORD your God. On that day no one in your household may do any work. This includes you, your sons and daughters, your male and female servants, your livestock, and any foreigners living among you. For in six days the LORD made the heavens, the earth, the sea, and everything in them; but on the seventh day he rested. That is why the LORD blessed the Sabbath day and set it apart as holy. Honor your father and mother. Then you will live a long, full life

in the land the LORD your God is giving you.
You must not murder.
You must not commit adultery.
You must not steal."

We're busy because we're under more pressure than ever before to provide for our families. According to the US Census Bureau, "The typical American family income was $53,657 in 2014, barely changed from $54,462 a year earlier." [5] Compare that to 1965, when the average (median) income was $6,900.[6] No wonder the Traditionalists and Baby Boomers wonder why we feel the pressure to work when the average income is so much larger. However, look at the average costs:

How Much Things Cost in 1965 compared to 2016 [7]

- House (median): $17,800 / $278,800
- Gas per Gallon: 31 cents / $2.36
- New Car: $2,650 / $33,560
- Loaf of Bread: 21 cents / $2.32

Let's get a little mathematical for a minute as we debunk this myth: Housing costs increased by $5,117 per year on average (from 1965 to 2016) whereas the average salary increased by $954 per year on average (from 1965 to 2014). So can we agree based on these approximate calculations that the cost of living has increased at a rate greater than the income generated? As a result, more women are busier than

5 Source: http://money.cnn.com/2015/09/16/news/economy/census-poverty-income/

6 Source: http://www2.census.gov/prod2/popscan/p60-049.pdf

7 Source: http://www.thepeoplehistory.com/1965.html; https://www.census.gov/construction/nrs/pdf/uspricemon.pdf; http://www.usatoday.com/story/money/cars/2015/05/04/new-car-transaction-price-3-kbb-kelley-blue-book/26690191/

ever before—it's a fact! They are balancing jobs and caring for families or carrying heavy loads while their spouses work longer hours in order to pay the bills. If we toss the divorce rate into the mix, at forty to fifty percent, then nearly one out of every two women are caring for their families as single moms.[8]

Busy isn't just a feeling. It's a reality. But if it becomes the reason why we can't connect, then we have a problem. Our busyness is actually a valid reason why we need community built around mentoring. But rather than it looking like coffee-dates, mentoring may need to take the shape of having a long talk while folding laundry. Instead of digging into Scripture together, it may require going for a walk and praying aloud together, in order to fit in exercise and time together. Unless the economy improves dramatically or the culture shifts in the direction of siestas, busy is here to stay, so why not look for ways to lighten the load with grace and creative solutions rather than heaping on guilt.

Myth 7: They have no sense of loyalty.

Out of all the myths, this may be the easiest to debunk because it's actually untrue across the board. The Gen X, Y, and Z generations are as loyal as they come, but they don't appear to be so because their loyalty must be earned. Ah yes, they've been burned, as children of divorce in a world marred by deception and deceit of every kind. They won't be quick to pledge allegiance to anyone or anything without integrity and credibility being first established. For example, when it comes to brands, this need for a personal connection has

---

8 Source: http://www.apa.org/topics/divorce/

become a foundation point in marketing.

> *"For Millennials, who may not have known a world without digital connectivity through social media, it's absolutely important that they feel like they're a part of something by engaging with the brands they like."* [9]

If this is how they approach what Millenials are willing to invest their money in, imagine how it shapes their mindset about relationships. In contrast, Traditionalists and Baby Boomers see loyalty from a totally different perspective. It's a "don't ask, just do it" mentality, where positions of authority and hierarchy carry weight, and you knew your place regardless of how you felt about your leader or boss or pastor or president.

When you look through the lens of loyalty that the older generation looks through, no wonder there is a breakdown in cross-generational relationships. However, I believe it's one of the easiest myths to overcome. What if the solution was found in seeking to work together, side by side, for the glory of God?

> Colossians 3:23 (NIV)
> *Whatever you do, work at it with all your heart, as working for the Lord, not for human masters ...*

Couldn't our sense of loyalty find more similarities rather than differences as we work together for God's purposes?

---

9 Source: http://www.millennialmarketing.com/2015/11/meet-the-millennial-digital-trends-and-authentic-brand-loyalty/

Myth 8: They don't care about Scripture.

Is it true that Millennials really don't care about the Scriptures and are falling away from their faith? According the latest study of the Pew Research Center in 2015, "the percentage of adults (ages 18 and older) who describe themselves as Christians has dropped by nearly eight percentage points in just seven years, from 78.4% in an equally massive Pew Research survey in 2007 to 70.6% in 2014."[10] It's hard to qualify those points in the grand scheme of things, and yet it's a drop none the less. But this drop doesn't mean that Scripture has lost relevancy in the lives of the younger generation.

According to Barna, "Of the practicing Christian Millennials who believe in absolute moral truth (71%), four in ten point to the Bible as the main source from which they have learned or discovered absolute moral truths and standards (39%). This far outpaces any other source, with church coming in second at only 16%, followed by parents at 14%." Additionally, "practicing Christian Millennials rank Bible reading as more important than church attendance (55% say Bible reading is more important), silence/solitude (50%), prayer (49%), worship (51%), acts of service (48%), communion (44%) and evangelism (42%)." [11]

For the Traditionalists and Baby Boomers, these statistics should be a fresh dose of hope and also an invitation to look for creative ways to pursue cross-centered mentoring. The Gen X, Y, and Zers, who are seeking to live according to the Word, crave these mentoring rela-

---

10 Source: http://www.pewforum.org/2015/05/12/americas-changing-religious-landscape/

11 Source: https://www.barna.org/barna-update/millennials/687-millennials-and-the-bible-3-surprising-insights#.VvA2fBIrLdc

tionships, even if the way they go about practicing their faith looks different. Worship may feel more like a rock concert. Bible reading may happen on an app. Bible studies may take place in a Facebook group. Yes, it's different, but not wrong, especially if the Word of God is being upheld as truth and the message of the gospel is going forth.

> John 17:17 (NIV)
> *Sanctify them by the truth; your word is truth.*

What hope there is in knowing that we can come around the Word as truth! Yes, that might mean we need to gather together in an eclectic, multi-generational way, bringing in old-time hymns and traditions along with modern twists and practices. Wouldn't that reflect the fullness of the body of Christ?

Embracing Our Part

Debunking the myths we believe about each generation is the first step in drawing toward each other and appreciating each other's differences. It's not a quick-fix process, but rather one that unfolds as we take stock of what we believe, how we're made by God, and the ways we can embrace our part in His kingdom purposes, cross-wired together one generation to another.

Reflection Questions

1. How do you fit into the generational stereotypes? Do you find yourself feeling like an old soul or more youthful than your generation? Can you pinpoint what experiences or relationships may have caused that to be the case?

2. Which of the myths have you believed? How has that impacted your relationships?

3. Of all the myths, which one(s) were somewhat convicting to you in regard to areas of prejudice or your own struggles? How will you go about resolving that issue in the future?

Impact Challenge

Write a letter to your (imaginary) great, great grandchildren. Tell them what you've learned through your life experiences thus far. Share with them about the pressures you feel, your fears of the future, and your hopes and dreams. When you finish, tuck it away for safe keeping while pursuing God about what rose up from your heart and mind. Ask Him to show you if there is anyone who you could come alongside now and encourage. Ask Him if there is anything that you are supposed to do in light of what you feel passionate about.

PART TWO

Eliminating Excuses

"Whatever the degree of involvement and however the relationship works itself out, the command is clear. Older women are to encourage and equip younger women to live for God's glory."

Susan Hunt

Spiritual Mothering: The Titus 2 Model for Women Mentoring Women

5

Battle for Truth

Would you agree that one of the main obstacles in cultivating mentoring relationships is in believing that it's truly possible? We are so good at coming up with a list of excuses that we end up erecting a wall around ourselves, really to protect our heart and pride from getting hurt, and yet the result is that we end up withdrawing from the very community we desire most of all. We don't reach toward one another for the fear of "what if?"

What if she thinks I'm too needy?

What if she feels like I'm outdated?

What if she doesn't want to spend time with me?

What if she's too busy?

What if I don't have the answers she's looking for?

What if I'm not wise enough?

What if I appear to be a hypocrite?

We "what if" ourselves into total isolation! We may find ourselves standing right next to that woman who could easily serve as a mentor, but are too afraid to even say hello out of fear of her response.

We sense a deep pain in that gal at the other end of the pew, but worry about what might be exposed if we reach toward her.

Our insecurities, fears, and festering wounds act as roadblocks to connecting at a heart level.

Quite frankly, sometimes we just don't know what to do with someone else's pain. And that's okay. There are times we simply can't respond to what we see in a tangible act ... but we can always pray! Other times, their issues are triggers for us, rising up pain from the past that's just not healthy in this season of life. I have a good friend who is in the process of healing with the help of counseling for trauma that's more than twenty-years old. She's well aware of how her thought-life influences her behavior and wants to deal with the junk that causes her to act in a way she wants to change. This investment in counseling is truly for the sake of her family, as she's totally invested in building a godly legacy for them. So, in this season of life, she has to guard herself against relationships that trigger the pain while she deals with healing from it. But by the grace of God, a time will come when her boundary lines can expand to include those who are also broken. I applaud her wisdom and discernment, knowing that her first priority is to get her heart and home in order before she reaches out to be mentored (and falls into the trap of creating a false god out of mother-figure) or mentor others.

Even when we are emotionally and spiritually healthy, we still have to battle for truth as the father of lies effortlessly worms his way into our secret thoughts and renders us utterly insecure about mentoring (or anything else, for that matter).

John 8:44
He was a murderer from the beginning. He has always hated the truth, because there is no truth in him. When he lies, it is consis-

tent with his character; for he is a liar and the father of lies.

The enemy simply looks at our lives, notes our weaknesses and fears, and offers up an excuse filled with half-truth, half lie. This is exactly what the serpent did in the Garden of Eden when he asked Eve, "Did God really say …?" (Genesis 3:1).

How many times are we caught in the same cycle of doubting God's plans and purposes, while believing the enemy's accusations? What begins with an innocent question of doubt opens the door to the deception. The enemy's purpose is clear, every time, as he sets out to steal, kill, and destroy us as well as our influence in this world.

John 10:10
The thief's purpose is to steal and kill and destroy. My purpose is to give them a rich and satisfying life.

The enemy's tactics are incredibly crafty and cunning, and almost always begin with a lie that spins into nothing short of the death of a dream, pursuit, purpose, or plan. Right now, our dream is to become women of influence, impacting the lives around us for the glory of God. We sense a need and want to respond, but first we need to do the hard work of battling the enemy of God with the truth! It is time to move out of the labyrinth of lies by confessing our thinking before God. That starts with owning our excuses, like …

I feel like a hypocrite, because of what I went through in the past.
I feel like I'm too young, in age or faith, to be able to speak into someone else's life.
I feel like I'm not smart enough or knowledgeable enough about Scripture to be able to mentor biblically.

I feel like I'm not gifted to serve as a mentor.

I feel like I don't have enough of me to give.

I feel like it is too risky emotionally, to get that invested only to end up dry, abandoned, hurt.

Which ones reflect your thinking? Maybe all? Or maybe an entirely different excuse? Or maybe, you think, "Hey, these aren't excuses. This is the facts, ma'am." Maybe you're right. There is truth in each statement. Or maybe, you're stuck in stinkin' thinkin' and it's time to move on. How about we find out?

Using Scriptures to Battle Excuses

Through looking at the Scriptures, we can discern which core excuses have become deeply embedded in our lives as we search the Word for an applicable truth. For example, the issue of feeling like a hypocrite can paralyze us from speaking into the lives of others. We may feel too afraid to give advice or offer direction, especially if we made a mistake in that particular area in the past. But as we look at Scripture, we can find the confidence through embracing the truth. For example:

Belief: I can't mentor, because I messed up by doing [fill in the blank].

Truth: Romans 3:23, "... for all have sinned and fall short of the glory of God ..." (ESV)

Application: I have made "this" mistake. Yes, I have sinned. But Scripture tells me all have sinned. If I believe that only people who haven't sinned could mentor, then no one could ever mentor. Therefore, the truth is that my sin does not prevent me from being qualified to mentor. The truth is that God redeems my sin through faith in Jesus Christ, and in Him, I can confidently go forth to mentor others.

Belief: I'm too young to mentor.
Truth: 1 Timothy 4:12, "Don't let anyone look down on you because you are young, but set an example for the believers in speech, in conduct, in love, in faith and in purity" (NIV).
Application: I'm only in my twenties, but if I can read the Scriptures and study life application principles, I can come alongside someone younger and impart that truth and His hope.

Belief: I don't have anything to give.
Truth: Colossians 3:12, "Therefore, as God's chosen people, holy and dearly loved, clothe yourselves with compassion, kindness, humility, gentleness and patience. Bear with each other and forgive one another if any of you has a grievance against someone. Forgive as the Lord forgave you. And over all these virtues put on love, which binds them all together in perfect unity."
Application: I might feel like I have nothing to give, but the truth is that with God working in me and through me, I can at least show compassion, kindness, humility, gentleness, and patience to others.

By applying Scripture truths to our excuses, we can move into the positions of influence God is leading us toward. So how about taking this principle and applying it to each of the excuses we'll consider in the following pages as we begin to put the application to work in everyday life?

Reflection Questions

1. What is your main excuse for not mentoring? Take time to jour-
    nal about this and seek the Lord in prayer in preparation for our
    further study about excuses.

2. Do you detect a pattern of thinking in your excuse(s)? If so,
    explain and look for the root of that particular issue.

3. Read the following passages in at least three different transla-
    tions, which you can find at Biblegateway.com, and jot down the
    one that stands out to you.

    •   John 10:10

    •   2 Corinthians 10:5

    •   Romans 12:2

Impact Challenge

Using John 10:10 as a framework for speaking with the Lord, take
time to reflect on the ways the enemy has sought to "steal, kill, and
destroy" in your life. But don't stay in that place for too long. Use
this time of reflection to gain clarity of vision, while shifting your
focus on the full life God promises. Ask Him what that looks like as
it's described in Scripture as well as a vision for your future. If you
feel comfortable, share your reflections with a sister in Christ and ask
for her honest feedback, accountability, and prayer support.

6

Hypocrite or Humble?

Hypocrite. It almost carries the sting of a curse word, don't you
think? To be called a hypocrite is a loaded accusation—one that is
usually spewed out of hurt stemming from a breach in trust. But
if we paused to consider what it means to be hypocrite, we'd soon
discover that sometimes such an accusation misses the mark, and
that our own fear of hypocrisy lacks an accurate understanding of the
definition:

> *hypocrite. noun.*
> *a person who pretends to have virtues, moral or religious beliefs,*
> *principles, etc., that he or she does not actually possess, espe-*
> *cially a person whose actions belie stated beliefs (dictionary.*
> *com).*

A hypocrite is a pretender—one whose actions belie stated beliefs.
So, would you call yourself a pretender, especially when it comes to
your faith? Are you not being authentic about who you really are as a
follower of Christ? My guess is that if you're taking the time to read
this book, pretending about your faith isn't your problem. However,
maybe you are a tad bit concerned that your actions don't line up
with your beliefs. Do you quote Scripture one minute, and act totally

against the principle the next? Have you made a policy decision based on your theology, but then don't live it out when push comes to shove? I know my actions don't always line up with my beliefs.

Action: I am harsher than a lawyer in a Hollywood case, even though I believe that kind words should come out of my mouth.
Belief: Proverbs 31:26, "She speaks with wisdom, and faithful instruction is on her tongue."

Action: I am overcome with jealousy over what others have, while telling my children to be grateful for what they have.
Belief: Colossians 3:15-16, "Let the peace of Christ rule in your hearts, since as members of one body you were called to peace. And be thankful. Let the message of Christ dwell among you richly as you teach and admonish one another with all wisdom through psalms, hymns, and songs from the Spirit, singing to God with gratitude in your hearts."

Action: I forget my identity one blink after reading Scripture as I scroll through social media, instead of remembering that I'm a co-heir with Christ and a child of God.
Belief: Romans 8:17, "Now if we are children, then we are heirs—heirs of God and co-heirs with Christ, if indeed we share in his sufferings in order that we may also share in his glory."

Action: I selfishly pursue the approval of others, instead of seeking the approval of God.
Belief: Galatians 1:10, "Am I now trying to win the approval of human beings, or of God? Or am I trying to please people? If I were still trying to please people, I would not be a servant of Christ."

Can you see yourself acting this way too? Do you behave in a way that is inconsistent with your beliefs? Oh friend, welcome to the club called "sinners saved by grace." In our flesh, we will all act in a way that is contrary to what we believe is right and true. But this is not hypocrisy. This is being human! We become hypocrites when we say that our wrong behavior is okay and make excuses about our sin. Hypocrisy is when we declare Scripture is true but we give up the fight in pursing right living. If we continue to do what we know is wrong, then yes, we are guilty of being hypocrites. But if we are walking before God, seeking His forgiveness, and determining to move in a new, right direction ... well then that makes us humble and perfectly positioned to mentor.

James 4:7-10 (NIV)
Submit yourselves, then, to God. Resist the devil, and he will flee from you. Come near to God and he will come near to you. Wash your hands, you sinners, and purify your hearts, you double-minded. Grieve, mourn and wail. Change your laughter to mourning and your joy to gloom. Humble yourselves before the Lord, and he will lift you up.

Well, think of who you want to follow—those who have it all together, or those who've learned the hard way? Who wouldn't want a humble woman serving as their mentor? Who knows what it means to be submitted to God. To resist the devil. To have their heart purified before the Lord. To move through seasons of grief and mourning into laughter and joy.

**We don't need perfect women leading us,
but humbly redeemed ones showing
us the way of Christ.**

The redemptive work of Christ speaks deeply to our hearts much more than a denial of sin-soaked mistakes. We need to be led, trained up, and impacted by women who have worked out their faith in real life, in real messes. We need to learn these lessons as we grow in vulnerable, transparent, multi-generational relationships together. But this doesn't mean we have to tout every sordid detail of our messy stories in order to be authentic and relatable.

The message isn't in the mess.
The message is in the story of redemption.

Stories are powerful teaching tools, my friend. Jesus used stories, as we see throughout the parables, to teach biblical truths, so we should feel free to follow His example. But it's the timing of telling our stories that can either lead to revelation or regret. There are times our stories are not yet ready to be told. If we're still in the throes of a trial or picking up the pieces of a life trauma, our message will sting of hurt and unanswered questions. God uses time (and often the support of a Christian counselor) to reveal His perspective and purposes. And yet, sometimes, decades later the wounds are still raw and the message is not yet ready, because it focuses on the gore instead of the God's glory. Friend, if you find yourself aware of an unhealed wound, I urge you to receive the promise Jesus gave to the woman at the well:

> Luke 7:48, 50
> *Then Jesus said to the woman, "Your sins are forgiven."*
> *... And Jesus said to the woman, "Your faith has saved you; go in peace."*

Your past doesn't need to define your present any longer. You can give up your shame to the Lord and walk in fresh forgiveness. And, as His healing takes over your heart, in due time, He'll give you the words to share your story in a way that gives glory to Him.

A redeemed woman need not be ashamed of a forgiven past.

We all have something in our pasts, and maybe even present, that we'd like to gloss over. And maybe, we should. That's been a hard truth for a girl who "wears her heart on her sleeve." I'm an authenticity nut, but I'm also learning that everything experienced and felt doesn't necessarily need to be shared in detail publicly … or at all. There are times when generalizations do more for giving forth gospel hope than painting the picture of redemption with all the gory details. So, checking my motives and assessing the state of my heart has become an important part of how I engage in not only mentoring, but also in how I communicate as a friend, writer, speaker, and even on social media.

When my words are critical, overflowing from a bitter soul and hurt heart, I know it's time to remain silent. While I may allude to a trial or share privately to some degree, neither a public platform nor a mentoring relationship is the place for a message.

Time gives room for healing, and healing brings perspective that infuses necessary grace into our stories.

And so, my friend, can we agree that our messes don't mean we're hypocrites? They just prove that we're humans in need of redemption, much like we see in the life of the apostle Paul. Wouldn't you be tempted to say that Paul was the biggest hypocrite of all time? He went from being a persecutor of Christ's followers to becoming persecuted for following Christ.

Paul's life was a mess before his conversion. He was a bold accuser of the followers of Jesus, and persecuted many for their faith. But once the scales on his eyes were removed, and his heart was totally yielded to the Lord, he became a great teacher and example for others. Because of Christ, Paul was equipped and qualified to teach, lead, and, yes, mentor. His past did not disqualify him. Neither does ours. Rather, his past made him all the more passionate about the work God called Him to:

1 Timothy 4:15-16 (NIV)
Here is a trustworthy saying that deserves full acceptance: Christ Jesus came into the world to save sinners—of whom I am the worst. But for that very reason I was shown mercy so that in me, the worst of sinners, Christ Jesus might display his immense patience as an example for those who would believe in him and receive eternal life.

Ephesians 3:7-9 (NIV)
I became a servant of this gospel by the gift of God's grace given me through the working of his power. Although I am less than the least of all the Lord's people, this grace was given me: to preach to the Gentiles the boundless riches of Christ, and to make plain to everyone the administration of this mystery, which for ages past was kept hidden in God, who created all things.

Paul refers to himself as the worst of all sinners and the least of all of God's people. Could he be any more humble? Could he be any less passionate as he proclaims the boundless riches of Christ and his mission to tell all? Paul is no more a hypocrite than you or I!

No matter how disqualified we might feel, in Christ we are re-qualified to serve as God-appointed mentors.

When we have been reconciled and redeemed by God, we are perfectly qualified to speak truth in the lives around us. That's because our goal isn't for those we mentor to follow us, but rather to become imitators of Christ (1 Corinthians 1:11). And, one last point on this matter of hypocrisy: Have you noticed that hearing about Paul's past has never tempted you to repeat his behavior? But isn't that a common excuse for not sharing with the next generation about our mistakes? We fear that if they know what we did, then what will that do for our authority? What permission might it give them to do the same thing? Ahem. Think about that for a minute. What if hearing about our foolish choices, described in broad strokes but with clear connection to the consequences, might motivate them into wiser decisions instead?

So would you agree with me that hypocrisy—when it comes to our faith and mentoring—isn't at all what we think it is? It's really only a threat from the enemy to keep us held back from positions of influence. It's time to tell him, "Enough is enough! I'm a redeemed child of God, equipped to share His good news always and everywhere!"

The Acceptable Excuse

At a number of times in my mentoring journey, I have stepped back from actively mentoring as well as speaking and teaching because my life circumstances prevented me from serving from the overflow of Christ within me. What do I mean by that? Well, imagine a water pitcher under a running faucet that is filled up to the brim and overflowing. It's so filled up, that there's plenty to pour out. The same is true of our personal lives—at times we are filled up to overflowing through our daily time with God and a life routine that gives space to breathe. Other times, we might feel like we're shriveling up and drying out, either because the stage and season is stretching us or we're in the midst of a trial.

In one particular season marked by many external trials that stirred up some painful parts of my past, the Lord made it quite clear that I was in no position to invest in others. My mentoring couch remained empty for nearly two years. Not only were girls not coming, I wasn't pursuing them nor making myself available for hosting ETC (a mentoring group that you can learn more about at http://www.moretobe.com/etc/).

At times, I feared my mentoring ministry was over, for good, and I wondered if I'd ever again have the joy of those special relationships. But I also recognized that I was unable to speak life and truth while being in the midst of my own mess. My words gave me away, as Matthew 12:34 conveys, "For whatever is in your heart determines what you say."

When our words reveal our hurting hearts, it is a clear indicator that we need to focus on personal healing instead of mentoring others.

As I sought help from the Lord as well as through Christian counseling, the deep wounds in my soul were healed by God and I was able to move forward into healthy mentoring relationships. Looking back, I can see how that season was marked by deep sanctification, bringing about a humility and compassion within me that I didn't have previously. Because of the pain endured and healing experienced, I brought to my mentoring relationships a new level of understanding, not only regarding the impact of sin but also the power of God's grace and freedom found in His forgiveness along with forgiving others.

Occasionally, we can embark on this healing journey with the Lord and continue to maintain our mentoring relationships. However, there are other situations in which the wounds run deep and lies have written over God's truth, requiring that we seek out help to move forward and heal.

One of the best things we can do for ourselves and those we love is take a step of faith into solid Christian counseling. Yes, I've had to do this multiple times! Christian counseling was a key way that God showed me the effects of my hardened and bitter heart, and opened my soul up to His transforming work (Ezekiel 36:26). It is only a myth that getting help proves weak faith.

Counseling is a tool God uses to heal broken and wounded souls.

It isn't a lifetime commitment, but it will have a lifetime benefit. Remember, it's about what He is doing in you and through you! So, my friend, there are times when mentoring ought to be put on hold. This is a decision I urge you to be sensitive toward and bathe in prayer, while seeking the counsel of godly advisors.

Romans 8:28
And we know that God causes everything to work together for the good of those who love God and are called according to his purpose for them.

We can always trust God's timing, both to reveal His purposes and to settle our uncertainty with His peace, as we wait on His prompting to step out and serve those around us.

Reflection Questions

1. Take time to read and reflect on Luke 7:36-50. Who do you identify with in the passage and why? How could you respond to someone who doesn't yet know the fullness of Christ's forgiveness?

2. How do you feel about sharing parts of your life and story with a mentor or mentee? Does it feel scary? Can you think about why you feel this way? Does it feel hard to know which parts to talk about and what to leave out? If so, take time to pray about this and speak with an older, wiser woman for direction.

3. Can you pinpoint situations from your past the enemy uses to call you a hypocrite? Take the time to seek the Lord's forgiveness and reconcile this past as you move toward living as a forgiven woman. If you find yourself stuck in this process, seek the help of your pastor or a Christian counselor.

Impact Challenge

Based on Matthew 12:34, how would you describe what is going on in your heart? Are there wounds festering and breeding bitterness? Is there unforgiveness and guilt or shame? Take note in the next few days on what you hear yourself saying, and seek the Lord in learning what it all means. Please don't feel shy about seeking professional help or the counsel of a pastor, either.

7

Walking in Wisdom

In our culture, where degrees and certificates determine credibility and authority, it is not surprising that many women feel it is not their place to speak into the lives of others. Is this "lack of credentials" something that holds you back too? Well, take heart, because cultivating biblical mentoring relationships isn't about being a seminary graduate or appointed women's ministry leader.

**Embracing multi-generational,
Christ-centered mentoring relationships
is about knowing the Word,
living it out, and passing it on.**

We don't need official qualifications to make us wisdom worthy women able to speak into the lives of others. But we do need to walk in the way of wisdom so that what we pass on is rooted in sound theology and accurate interpretation of Scripture. What does this mean? Well, let's think of it from a super simplistic perspective. If a six-year-old girl came to you and said she wanted to make a peanut butter and jelly sandwich, what would you say to her? You might think, "Well, I'll take care of that. You're too young to figure it out all by yourself. You can't reach the jelly in the fridge. You won't be able to open the lid on the peanut butter. And you'll probably make a sticky mess all over yourself and the counter." This approach accomplishes the goal … the girl gets her PB&J. But there is also another approach.

Maybe, instead, you'd get everything out and set up on the counter, pull up a stool, and let her do the assembling of the sandwich. Yes, it might be messy, but it's an attainable task for a six year old. Or, maybe, if you don't mind messes and can handle some amount of risk, you'd be willing to walk her through the steps verbally, tell her where to find the necessary ingredients and tools, and allow her to conquer the task all by herself. She might succeed. She might fail. But through the process, she'll learn something about her abilities and grow in confidence about her abilities as you put your trust in her.

How does this all relate to mentoring and the wisdom we need from God? Well, like that little girl, we need to want it—wisdom, that is. We need to ask God for it! Yes, it's that simple!

James 1:5 (MSG)
If you need wisdom, ask our generous God, and he will give it to you. He will not rebuke you for asking.

We get to ask God for the wisdom we need and we also have the opportunity to pursue the wisdom He's already made available to us through the Word. But, will we simply wait for others to come along and do the learning for us—maybe through listening to sermons and completing Bible studies? It's not a bad option. Actually, it's a great first step. But at some point, we need to take more ownership in the process. We'll need to decide that being spoon-fed isn't good enough, and instead, we'll need to crack open our Bibles and make time for pouring through the Word. We'll need to wrestle out principles and study the Scriptures at a deeper level, while seeking the Holy Spirit to give us the wisdom we crave. Yes, gaining wisdom is a process that requires both willingness and devotion.

God equips us to mentor through giving us the wisdom we seek and the Word we need!

The Message translation of James 1:5 puts it this way, "If you don't know what you're doing, pray to the Father. He loves to help. You'll get his help, and He won't be condescended to when you ask for it." We don't need all the answers to life's great questions in order to validate our authority to mentor. We simply need to know where to find the answers: from God and through the Scriptures. This is summed up perfectly in Colossians:

> Colossians 3:16
> *Let the message about Christ, in all its richness, fill your lives. Teach and counsel each other with all the wisdom he gives. Sing psalms and hymns and spiritual songs to God with thankful hearts.*

Through our relationship with Christ and time spent in the Word, we are equipped by God to confidently and boldly mentor others. So what next steps should you take to grow as a student of the Word so you have an overflowing well of wisdom to pour forth?

A Word about Our Words

As we think about the wisdom we need to guide our mentoring relationships, there's another factor worth considering. Did you know that God holds us accountable not only for the way we live but also for the words we speak?

Matthew 12:36-37
And I tell you this, you must give an account on judgment day for every idle word you speak. The words you say will either acquit you or condemn you.

Oh yes, we will give an account to God for every word we speak! Oye! Does that make you panic like it does me? As my father used to say, "Loose lips sink ships." If that's as true, as this verse from Matthew supports, I'm drowning. My quickness to speak combined with my temper is a horrible combination when it comes to being accountable for what comes out of my mouth. Ah, but my track record is not beyond God's forgiveness. My carelessly spoken words are still within the covering of God's grace, but that doesn't mean I can abuse it. It's a both/and—BOTH being cognizant of my propensity to sin with my mouth while guarding my words carefully as I heed the leading of the Holy Spirit, AND quickly seeking God's forgiveness when I've not acted wisely.

Being wise with our words is a skill we have to exercise as mentors!

Yes, it means I have to slow down my mouth to be on track with the Spirit and be more thoughtful about listening rather than speaking. It's a skill that comes with experience, but that doesn't mean wisdom is only given to the old.

Wisdom Isn't Only for the Old

Do you believe that to be wise you have to be old? Or do you believe that only the older amongst us are qualified to mentor? I can't tell you the number of times I've heard women confess that they didn't feel old enough to mentor. It goes right along with the mindset about not feeling wise enough. But, as I've challenged you to think about the source of wisdom—God's Word and the revelation of the Holy Spirit—I also want to stretch your thinking about the "right" age for mentoring.

We don't need to be old to be wise, nor do we need to be old to mentor.

But we do need to be willing to speak into someone else's life, sometimes when we're pursued and other times when we're asked.

I remember one time asking an older friend, Debbie, who had a beautifully maturing teenage daughter, about her parenting style. I saw her as "older and wiser," and although we had no formal meeting time together, I felt comfortable enough to seek out her advice. I really wanted to know how she managed to raise a polite, intelligent, creative, thoughtful girl in the midst of a culture that says it is impossible to do so in this day and age. Instead of giving me parenting advice, however, she introduced me to Anne Ortlund's book, *Disciplines of a Beautiful Woman.* Ortlund's trilogy literally changed my entire perspective on becoming the woman God intended—especially as a mother, wife, and mentor—and radically influenced my approach to mothering but also mentoring. Ortlund helped me to see myself not only as a mother, but as a disciple of Christ commissioned to disciple others, beginning first with my children. Her simple teaching on discipleship awakened in me a brand new confidence in being able to learn Scripture, live it out, and share it with others.

As I sought to be a student of the Word, I noticed that it was natural to overflow what I was learning in organic times with my children.

In essence, I was discipling them by sharing the Word, but from a mentoring perspective through doing life together in the context of our relationship, and not in a formal Bible study.

This unintentional mentoring is exactly what occurred in a multi-generational way for my family through our interactions with our babysitters. From the time our firstborn was three months old, we took advantage of our boarding school community and brought into our home a teenage girl to babysit for our weekly date night. In the early years, I would pick a sitter who seemed to need a little bit of special attention, knowing my own kids would fill up her love tank, and hopefully, I would have a chance to encourage her personally. These conversations were steeped in the Word spoken, not formally taught, as we discussed every aspect of her life and I shared my own challenges and "ah-has" with her. I was mentoring, one teen girl at a time, when I had the time, even though I was only in my late twenties. One might say that's not old enough to be a mentor, and yet, that's exactly what I was doing.

As our children grew, however, we became more intentional about looking for sitters who demonstrated tenderness to our children as well as a sweet balance of maturity, teachability, and sensitivity about their influence on our kids. When our oldest daughter was entering the later part of elementary school, we were blessed with two precious young women who had a heart for God, an understanding of the times, and a deep love for our children. They were also eager to be mentored, and would stick around after we returned home from our date night to chat about our children as well as share about their personal lives. What is amazing, however, was that as I was mentoring these two teen girls, they were also mentoring my girls. They used their babysitting opportunity to speak into my daughters' lives, endearing their hearts to God's ways. By doing so, they became mentors at the young age of sixteen, using what I taught them each week to respond to the needs of the ones they delighted in mentoring.

Through witnessing our teenage babysitters speak truth and wisdom into our lives (yes, even mine), I am convinced that age cannot disqualify you from mentoring.

> 1 Timothy 4:12
> *Don't let anyone think less of you because you are young. Be an example to all believers in what you say, in the way you live, in your love, your faith, and your purity.*

You can never be too young to impact others. You simply need to be sure you're taking in God's Word so you overflow with His wisdom. I beg you to not use the "I'm too young excuse" and miss out on the opportunity to be part of the ripple effect of one generation impacting another.

Reflection Questions

1. Do you struggle with the fear of not being wise enough to mentor? If so, have you asked the Lord to impart His wisdom on you? If not, would you be willing to stop right now and pray about this matter?

2. Would you be willing to invest time in studying Scripture, so that the Word may dwell richly in you? If so, what first step could you take in that direction today?

3. Is there a practical way you could informally mentor others?

Impact Challenge

Can you take a minute to look at your life to see if you've experienced informal mentoring? Jot down those moments and give thanks to the Lord for them. Are there younger women who could use your influence? Write down their names and pray about how God might use you. Would you like to seek out a mentor? Who might you ask? Pray about this!

8

Embracing Our Wiring

Have you ever noticed how some women are simply great encouragers, finding opportunities to express kind and uplifting words at just the right moment? How about those women who seem to be able to pull off hosting a dinner party for forty without fussing a bit over the details? Maybe your best friend never feels too tired to serve in the nursery or organize another craft for her child's class. Or maybe your mom was always able to keep her home tidy and put together while your eclectic space is crying out for a deep cleaning.

As you look around the circle of women in your life, are you left wondering, what's wrong with me? How am I gifted? What's up with my personality? When will I ever get to fulfill my God-given calling like the way she does? Oh my, friend, you are not alone in this cycle of defeat and despair. I can't think of anything more insidious in our culture than comparison leading to a sense of insecurity and lack of worth.

Our female hearts, ripe for affirmation and approval, fall into the comparison trap in a desperate search for significance.

In the process, we not only lose our joy, but we also miss out on the opportunity to join God in His work doing what He made us to do. When we are busy looking at everyone else, it's impossible to appreciate what we have. Social media, of course, doesn't help this one bit. We are more aware than ever of the successes of others. We witness launches, accomplishments, awards, and celebrations like never before. Doesn't it feel at times like everyone else has something big happening in their lives, while we can't find a single positive thing to post about? But really, we're only looking at the highlights and missing the reality of lows we all experience.

Wouldn't you agree that our tendency to compare keeps us from contentment? Morever, it festers insecurities that hold us back from stepping out as mentors and seeking mentoring. Maybe that's why the Scriptures are not only filled with reminders to not be jealous, envious, and greedy, but also to focus on the opposite behavior: Thankfulness.

> 1 Chronicles 16:4
> *Give thanks to the Lord, for he is good; his love endures forever.*

> Psalm 100:4
> *Enter his gates with thanksgiving and his courts with praise; give thanks to him and praise his name.*

> Colossians 3:15
> *Let the peace of Christ rule in your hearts, since as members of one body you were called to peace. And be thankful.*

> Colossians 4:2
> *Devote yourselves to prayer, being watchful and thankful.*

Hebrews 12:28

Therefore, since we are receiving a kingdom that cannot be shaken, let us be thankful, and so worship God acceptably with reverence and awe …

1 Thessalonians 5:18

… give thanks in all circumstances; for this is God's will for you in Christ Jesus.

1 Timothy 6:6

But godliness with contentment is great gain.

As it's written in Colossians 3:10, we've got to put off the old self—our sinful behaviors—and put on the right way of living. So imagine, what would your life look like if you were thankful for what the Lord has given you and the way He made you, rather than looking at what others have and are capable of accomplishing as they operate in their God-given wiring? Maybe you were never meant to host a dinner party for forty. Or serve in the nursery at church. Or keep a tidy house. God might be calling you to something all together different. Like writing a novel about God's redemptive work. Or leading an organization of five hundred with a Christ-centered example. Or caring for five little ones under foot.

God is calling you to embrace this life and the way He marvelously made you.

Where you are today is exactly where God wants you to be, using the gifts and talents He's sown into your life in the roles you're filling. But maybe your roles don't feel satisfying. Maybe you're ready to embrace the next best yes, but God has you hemmed in for a purpose you've yet to uncover.

I remember those sleepless nights with my twins as the hardest ones I had to embrace. Even though I was head-over-heels in love with these unexpected bundles, I was weary and still coping with my life being rerouted. Before they were born, I was managing quite well caring for my older daughters and loving being out of the diaper bag stage. My mentoring ministry was just starting to take shape, and I actually began blogging when the twins were only six months old. Being "trapped" at home gave me time to write, while they napped. However, as they became more active and my writing turned into a passion for something more significant, I ended up in the middle of what we call in life coaching a core value conflict. What I valued as important—being an intentional and invested mom AND also actively using my gifts and passion in ministry—couldn't all fit within the same schedule. There simply wasn't enough time to do both well. So I had to lay one down.

Yes, my writing dreams were pushed to the back burner, but that didn't mean the gifting God wired up in me was useless. I continued to write, as I could, while also seeking ways to serve others, especially as a mentor, whenever I had the time and energy to do so. From the outside, nothing formal was happening in my life other than motherhood. But on the inside, God was working in me, growing me, honing my gifts, and preparing me for the next season of serving Him while I embraced His calling on my life in that moment. What would it look like for you to do the same?

Finding Our Place in Our Purpose

We each have a God-given purpose that is tied to our God-given wiring. What do I mean by that? Well, I believe wholeheartedly that the way God designed us individually is meant for a corporate purpose.

Our temperaments, talents, experiences, and spiritual gifts all come together within the sovereignty of God's plan to be used by Him in fulfilling His broader purposes. I believe His kindness is such that He lets us choose to embrace His design and join Him in His work. He won't force it upon us, but rather He invites us to participate in His work by submitting our will and our gifts to Him.

The Word describes this process as each part being used for the benefit of the whole body of Christ, as it's explained in 1 Corinthians:

> 1 Corinthians 12:4-7
> *There are different kinds of spiritual gifts, but the same Spirit is the source of them all. There are different kinds of service, but we serve the same Lord. God works in different ways, but it is the same God who does the work in all of us. A spiritual gift is given to each of us so we can help each other.*

Do you see the key word in this passage: Different! It's used three distinct times:

Different gifts.
Different service.
Different ways.

In the original Greek, the word is *diairesis*, which actually means "varieties."[12] What a lovely concept to embrace as we look at the manifestation of the spiritual gifts in our lives.

There ought to be beautiful and dynamic variety in how we live and serve for the glory of God!

---

12 Source: https://www.blueletterbible.org/lang/lexicon/lexicon.cfm?Strongs=G1243&t=NIV

God's creativity is limitless but purposeful! He's made each one of us unique for the sake of helping each other. What good would we be if we were all the same? This truth, my friend, is why it's so important to see our valuable place in community. It's why each one of us can confidently step into mentoring relationships, because there is no one person out there who is the perfect fit. There's not one single, perfect, ideal way to mentor. There's no gifting that makes a person any more qualified than another.

You don't need to have someone else's gifts to mentor. You need to have yours.

God did not clone us. He didn't make one model good and another bad. He made us different and valuable. He made us to use our gifts and to be stretched beyond them. We are created in the image of God, and we can bring His purposes through freely using our gifts and talents to every relationship. Every mentoring relationship, therefore, will look different, based on the God-designed uniqueness of each person. And, ultimately, the fact that we each have a unique position within the body of Christ also implies we ought to have many mentors, because one woman could never meet all our needs to be trained up. What a freeing thought! We can give up looking for the perfect mentor or striving to become one because we really do need a circle of mentors to serve us and for us to serve!

Uncovering Your Wiring

Maybe all this reflection about our God-given wiring sounds wonderful, but leaves you wondering, "How do I figure out mine?" Well, there's a couple of different approaches you can take, depending on how much time you want to invest in the process.

Option 1: Simple Evaluation

Take time to reflect on your life as you answer these questions. When you finish, see if you can connect the dots in order to shape a vision for how God might use your gifts and passions in serving a particular type of person as a mentor.

1. What would I say I'm good at? Would others agree?
2. What would I say I am not good at doing? Would others agree?
3. What have I done in the past that has given me joy or made me feel alive?
4. What types of groups of people do I enjoy working with?
5. What types of groups of people would I rather not work with?
6. What tasks do I enjoy doing?
7. What tasks drive me nuts?
8. What settings do I feel the most comfortable in?
9. What settings make me uncomfortable?
10. If I could do anything with my time and gifts, I would like to do the following…

Option 2: Free Online Assessments

In addition to answering the questions in Option 1, take the time to do a selection of online assessments. Compare and contrast the results as you pinpoint what ways God may desire to use you as a mentor, and also how your personality impacts the way you relate to others.

For example, I have an extroverted friend, Jen, who flits from person to person at every women's gathering. She comes home feeling "fed" socially, yet for all the women she talked with, she still craves authentically deep connections. The problem is, she doesn't know who to pursue because her social nature doesn't want to focus on just one person. In contrast, my other friend, Liz, is an introvert, and she refuels alone, but doesn't want to be entirely isolated. Large social gatherings that require small talk not only overwhelm her, it can utterly deplete her reserves. So, for an introverted momma of littles, attending a playgroup or MOPS (Mothers of Preschoolers, mops.org) gathering can totally derail her. Yet, that doesn't change her need for mentoring, right?

As you explore the personality assessments, keep these questions in mind:

1. How do my strengths and weaknesses play out in relationships?
2. What types of social environments am I best suited for?
3. Would I do better in one-on-one relationships or in a group setting?
4. What traits in others really bother me and need a dose of grace?

Personality Assessments and Results

- 16 Personalities based on the JUNG Test: http://www.16personalities.com/
- Explanation of MBTI Results: https://www.cpp.com/products/mbti/index.aspx
- Descriptions of Personalities: http://www.truity.com/view/types
- JUNG Test: http://similarminds.com/jung_word.html
- Visual of JUNG Results: https://www.cpp.com/contents/type-heads.aspx

- DISC Test: http://www.123test.com/disc-personality-test/
- Spiritual Gifts at ChurchGrowth: http://www.churchgrowth. org/
- Spiritual Gift Test: http://www.spiritualgiftstest.com/

Option 3: Professional Assessments

If you'd like to go a step further in understanding your God-given wiring and gaining valuable feedback, the Highlands Assessment Battery (HAB) is an excellent option. The HAB is a method, a model, and a process of self-discovery that enables you to look at your whole-life picture and pinpoint your God-given abilities and personal style as it pertains to interacting with others. The battery reveals how you problem solve, where you get your energy from, and how you connect with others, providing you with a framework for approaching relationships, educational studies, and career pursuits. You can learn more about the HAB at http://www.moretobe.com/highlands-assessment-tool/

Not only will you grow personally as you embrace this process of understanding your God-given wiring, but you'll also gain tremendous insight on how to relate to others. And that insight will prove incredibly beneficial as you seek to cultivate multi-generational mentoring relationships.

Find Yourself, Find Your Excuse

When it comes right down to it, mentoring is about living as a disciple of Christ. Even if we have fought hard against all the excuses we've looked at thus far, there still may be more derailing you from answering the call to mentor...derailing you from experiencing the life God intended.

This "one more excuse" is the biggest of them all because it is completely and utterly yours. Only you will be able to uncover it and call it out, because it is so deeply rooted in your very own variety of insecurity, usually layered in jealousy and masked by a bit of perfectionism. Only you will be able to see its ugly presence, as you pause to listen to the voice of doubt whispering defeat into your mind. You might hear it in that moment when you look outward instead of upward, and fall onto the slippery slope of "well, she has ... does ... is" or find yourself repeating the mantra of "I don't ... won't ... can't ... will never ...". So as you think about the unique way God has designed your life and begin to embrace His purposes, I urge you to consider this one important question: What is your but?

But my house is too small ...

But my home isn't pretty enough ...

But my family is such a mess ...

But I am not beautiful enough to stand in front of people ...

But what about the way I struggle with knowing what to say ...

But I know I'm not organized enough to be helpful ...

But my life is in chaos...

But if I were married ...

But if I weren't divorced ...

But if I had my own children ...

But if my prodigal child would come home ...

But I don't think she would ever want to talk to me ...

But ...

Friend, when you pinpoint your excuse, in light of all that you've learned about yourself, you'll be able to move right through it and embrace the opportunities before you to mentor. It's all about demolishing the enemy's lie with the truth! So how about owning your "but" and taking it before the Lord to ask Him what He has to say about it?

Reflection Questions

1. Do you struggle with comparison and discontentment? With insecurity and the need for approval? If so, what is God speaking to your heart about this struggle and how to break free from it?

2. Take a few minutes to read all of 1 Corinthians 12 and Romans 12. What instructions do you take away from these passages for using your gifts and stretching beyond them?

3. What do you see as the God-given gifts you bring to the body of Christ? And how could you use those gifts in a practical way in a mentoring relationship?

4. What "but" is standing in your way? What does God have to say about it?

Impact Challenge

Take the time to complete one or all of the three proposed options for discovering your temperament and spiritual gifting. As you embrace this process, spend time in prayer, asking God to give you the eyes to see His wonderful work within you. Continue in prayer after the assessments, asking God to show you the ways He wants to use you, according to His design, in mentoring relationships.

PART THREE

M.E.N.T.O.R.

Are you ready to dive into the practical side of
cultivating biblical mentoring relationships? In the
short chapters to follow, we'll unpack six simple
principles for mentoring designed to equip you to
foster healthy, burden-free relationships using the
acronym, M.E.N.T.O.R.

M	meeting
E	encouraging
N	noticing
T	training
O	offering
R	responding

As you turn the page, remember to embrace these
steps of mentoring within much grace, looking for
the application principles in light of the way God has
uniquely wired you and orchestrated your life to join
Him in His work.

9

Meeting

SKETCHING OUT THE PLAN

The "M" in "mentor" stands for meeting together, because to develop a mentoring-rich relationship, you'll need to spend time together. Of course, this will take on a different format depending upon the nature of your relationship.

If you're seeking to mentor your daughter, you might look for opportunities to speak into her life in your normal routine, such as that long car ride to an after-school commitment or during morning devotions together. However, if your desire is be more intentional or to reach out to someone outside your family, setting forth expectations and boundaries around meeting together is essential.

Prayer Covering

Before committing to a mentoring relationship, set aside time to pray for the relationship and the Lord's direction. Make it a priority to also pray before and after every meeting time, asking the Lord to ordain every word that will be spoken and every experience shared, as well as to bind up the work of the enemy.

Time Expectations

As you consider what you hope to gain out of the mentoring relationship, take the time to consider your availability both in terms of hours and months.

- Are you interested in a weekly meeting or monthly?
- Would you prefer it to last only one hour or up to two?
- How many weeks or months in a row do you want to meet for?
- Would a phone call meeting work instead?

In some cases, meeting face-to-face isn't possible for a mentoring relationship. If this is your situation, decide on what other communication option is viable, such as phone, text messaging, Skype, Facebook chat, Voxing, or email. Think outside the box to find what works best for both of you.

Location Destination

Do you have a place in mind that you'd like to meet? Is it a convenient location? Is it free from distractions? A home is a great setting and allows for intimacy and creativity, but if people are bouncing around, it might be better to opt for a walk or getting together at a favorite coffee place. And, if you're the type who feels you must clean up to have someone over, a home destination can quickly become a stressful experience.

Plan and Purpose

It is a great idea to set a tentative plan for what you'll be doing in your time together. If you don't have a purpose for your mentoring relationship, it is easy to grow discouraged and distracted. Consider these options for your mentoring purpose:

- Prayer
- Accountability
- Study of Scripture
- Discussing a particular issue
- Reading a book together
- Honing in on a life skill, such as cooking
- Exercising with time to connect before or after

Boundaries

When a mentoring relationship takes on a formal meeting time, it becomes very important to set boundaries to avoid bitterness and conflict later on. Together, you should determine and agree upon the following:

- length of each meeting, such as forty-five minutes to an hour
- how often you will meet, such as once a week or every other week
- how long you'll meet for, such as three to six months
- purpose of your meeting time
- confidentiality, as in what is shared is kept private unless it is a matter of emotional or physical crisis that requires medical or legal attention
- commitment expectation, such as cancellations must be

twenty-four hours in advance
- a date to reevaluate and set a new mentoring course

Permission Slip

If you will be mentoring a young person, be sure to receive her parent(s) or guardian's permission. It is wise to inform them of your intentions and request the support of your mentoring relationship. In most cases, they will be delighted to have your investment of time and love in their child's life.

Meeting with your mentee will become one of those treasured opportunities as you see God's hand orchestrating the details of your lives and weaving your stories together.

Reflection Questions

1. How do these ideas redefine the nuts and bolts of mentoring in your mind?

2. Which of these steps will come naturally to you?

3. Which one(s) make you uncomfortable and will present a challenge?

10

Encouraging

IN WORD AND DEED

The "E" in "mentor" is to remind us to *encourage* one another through words and actions that glorify God. The way we go about encouraging each another in our mentoring relationships will be unique to our combination of gifts, talents, experiences, personality, and love language, so there is no single best practice when it comes to encouragement. Rather, it's a reflection of our God-given wiring working in tandem.

Encourage Practically

As you look for opportunities to encourage one another, it will be helpful to begin by understanding each other's temperament and gifting. So, if you haven't already done the personality and spiritual gifts assessments for yourself, this would be a great time to do it together. After you complete the assessments, spend time discussing your results so you can learn how to serve one another best and also discover how to communicate with a greater measure of sensitivity for each other's God-given conversation style.

In addition to the personality and spiritual gift assessments, it's also worth looking at your love language, as taught by Gary Chapman (http://www.5lovelanguages.com/profile/). Knowing how each other prefers to give and receive love will offer insights for connecting in the most effective way. For example, what do you think is your preference for receiving and giving love?

Words

Do you like to have the opportunity to talk? Are you encouraged by words of affirmation? How often do you need to connect verbally to be confident about your relationship?

Time

Do you feel loved by time spent together? How much time is enough? How much is too little?

Gifts

Do you respond to gifts? Does the price tag matter? Is it the personalization that grabs your heart?

Touch

How do you feel about being hugged? Do you crave a physical expression of love, like a touch on the hand or back?

Actions

What actions demonstrate love to you? Are you looking to co-labor with others in a project? Does serving feel like love?

There is also another side of encouraging from a practical perspective that is all about meeting the need in the moment, regardless of personality type, spiritual gifting, or love language. While the results to all those assessments are helpful for cultivating a new relationship, sometimes opportunities to serve as a mentor are circumstantial. Consider the situation described in Luke 1, when Mary went to Elizabeth:

Luke 1:39-42 (NIV)
At that time Mary got ready and hurried to a town in the hill country of Judea, where she entered Zechariah's home and greeted Elizabeth. When Elizabeth heard Mary's greeting, the baby leaped in her womb, and Elizabeth was filled with the Holy Spirit. In a loud voice she exclaimed: "Blessed are you among women, and blessed is the child you will bear!"

Elizabeth and Zechariah graciously offered Mary a safe haven for the remainder of her pregnancy. What I love about this picture is that it wasn't only shelter they offered, but a blessing rooted in authentic love. Elizabeth received Mary with open arms and spoke words of life over her. Who wouldn't want that type of greeting and embrace? This beautiful older woman extending herself to a younger one— both reaching toward each other with humility and love. Isn't this what mentoring should look like?

There's another aspect of mentoring that jumps out at me as I consider the relationship between Mary and Elizabeth. While they knew each other (they were family), they were not a regular part of each other's lives since they did not live in the same town. Drawing together was a result of circumstance and for such a time as this, which is often the case in mentoring!

Encourage Biblically

As you think of practical ways to encourage the women you're mentoring or even being mentored by, it's worth your time to take your cues from Scripture. The Word is steeped in rich instruction on how to navigate through relationships. God is gracious to remind us how to speak to one another, serve each other, and season our conversations with words of encouragement. Simply by applying these few Scripture passages, you can set the tone for your relationship:

What should we talk about?

Whatever is true, honorable, right, pure, lovely, admirable, excellent, and worthy of praise.

Philippians 4:8-9
And now, dear brothers and sisters, one final thing. Fix your thoughts on what is true, and honorable, and right, and pure, and lovely, and admirable. Think about things that are excellent and worthy of praise. Keep putting into practice all you learned and received from me—everything you heard from me and saw me doing. Then the God of peace will be with you.

How should I express godly love?

Love is an action, not a feeling.

1 Corinthians 13 (MSG)
The Way of Love. If I speak with human eloquence and angelic ecstasy but don't love, I'm nothing but the creaking of a rusty gate. If I speak God's Word with power, revealing all his mysteries and making everything plain as day, and if I have faith that says to a mountain, "Jump," and it jumps, but I don't love, I'm nothing. If I give everything I own to the poor and even go to the stake to be burned as a martyr, but I don't love, I've gotten nowhere. So, no matter what I say, what I believe, and what I do, I'm bankrupt without love. Love never gives up. Love cares more

for others than for self. Love doesn't want what it doesn't have. Love doesn't strut, Doesn't have a swelled head, Doesn't force itself on others, Isn't always "me first," Doesn't fly off the handle, Doesn't keep score of the sins of others, Doesn't revel when others grovel, Takes pleasure in the flowering of truth, Puts up with anything, Trusts God always, Always looks for the best, Never looks back, But keeps going to the end. Love never dies. Inspired speech will be over some day; praying in tongues will end; understanding will reach its limit. We know only a portion of the truth, and what we say about God is always incomplete. But when the Complete arrives, our incompletes will be canceled.

How should I use the Word?

Use the Word for correction, rebuke, and encouragement, but with great patience and careful instruction.

2 Timothy 4:2
Preach the Word; be prepared in season and out of season; correct, rebuke and encourage—with great patience and careful instruction.

Truth without grace is condemnation. Grace without truth is compromise.

How should I approach conversations and my reactions?

Be quick to listen. Slow to speak. Slow to get angry.

James 1:19

Understand this, my dear brothers and sisters: You must all be quick to listen, slow to speak, and slow to get angry.

What should I do when hurts and wounds come up?

Respond with tenderhearted mercy, kindness, humility, gentleness, and patience. Pursue and promote forgiveness. Put on love and the peace of Christ. And be thankful.

Colossians 3:12-15
Since God chose you to be the holy people he loves, you must clothe yourselves with tenderhearted mercy, kindness, humility, gentleness, and patience. Make allowance for each other's faults, and forgive anyone who offends you. Remember, the Lord forgave you, so you must forgive others. Above all, clothe yourselves with love, which binds us all together in perfect harmony. And let the peace that comes from Christ rule in your hearts. For as members of one body you are called to live in peace. And always be thankful.

There are so many wonderful ways you can practically and biblically encourage one another in a mentoring relationship. Can you see how these principles can go both ways—from older to younger, and younger to older? That's because these are solid biblical principles that ought to guide all our relationships. So regardless of who you're connected to right now, how about putting even half these biblical principles into action this week? Imagine parenting from this perspective? Or loving your husband with these principles? And even engaging with your coworkers with a determination to encourage biblically? Wow, isn't that a holy pursuit that will leave a lasting impact!

Reflection Questions

1. How can your awareness of your love language integrate into your current relationships, in addition to the ways you mentor and receive mentoring?

2. Can you think of one action step that would be received as encouragement for each of the five different love languages?

3. Looking at the Scripture passages, jot down a list of action words and descriptive adjectives to create a checklist for your mentoring relationships.

   • Philippians 4:8-9

   • 1 Corinthians 13

   • 2 Timothy 2:4

   • James 1:19

   • Colossians 3:12-15

11

Noticing

CURIOSITY AND QUESTIONS

The "N" in "mentor" stands for *noticing* what's going on in the other person. Noticing isn't simply about looking at her from the outside—it's also about paying attention to her whole being as you look beyond the surface. It's about hearing what is said and also learning how to read between the lines.

Noticing requires observation skills, which for some, isn't as natural as others. For example, on the Highlands Ability Battery (an assessment that considers personality type, natural abilities, driving abilities, and learning channels), my observation skills come in at 99 percent! Do you know what that means? Well, I have the ability to take in what is going on with a person, as my mind absorbs all that is being communicated through words and actions. It's an asset most of the time, as what I see enables me to reach out to meet a need or ask a question.

Of course, the downside of being highly observant is that I'm always taking in information, and that can be exhausting. I feel heart-deep simply by what I see, even if the words aren't spoken. If I'm with a large crowd, like at a speaking engagement, it's not only a sea of women before me. From the platform, I can see their stories in their eyes, their body language, and how they interact with each other as well as their response to what I'm saying. I could go home totally wiped out as I processed what I perceived as a result of what I've observed. However, the Lord's been gracious in showing me that I get to take it all in and then intercede in prayer on their behalf. Ah, that is the gift of noticing—being able to respond as a coworker of Christ in the way He leads.

Being able to respond to the needs of those we're mentoring, and sometimes, being mentored by, requires intentionality and a keen ear to listen to both the words spoken and the heart hidden. Whether it is face to face, over the phone, or through text or email, actively listen and look for opportunities to come alongside, encourage, pray, and respond to each other's practical needs. For example:

- Listen for dates, such as anniversaries and birthdays of loved ones, that you can mark on your calendar and remember to send a card, email, or text message.
- Make a note of upcoming events that need extra prayer and support, such as an interview, conference, travel, or event, and be sure to call on that day.
- Discern if she is overwhelmed by going someplace alone or getting ready for an event and offer her companionship.
- Prod beyond her words, asking questions to reveal the true state of her heart, and then offer to pray together.
- How does she look today? Run down, distracted, stressed? Put your agenda for your meeting time on hold and ask how she's doing. Be willing to change up your time to give her some refreshment.

We all like to be noticed. Especially when it comes from a heart of compassion and concern. Noticing is key to offering personalized and practical encouragement.

It's not about noticing and fixing. It's about noticing and yielding to God working through us in response to what we see.

In some cases, that might be prayer. It could also be choosing to serve a practical need. Sometimes it requires stepping back and other times leaning in. Often, noticing requires asking open-ended, thought-provoking question, like the ones used by life coaches. An open-ended question doesn't lead to a yes or no answer. Instead, it requires an explanation. For example:

Close-ended
Question: Do you want ice cream?
Answer: Yes, I want ice cream.

Open-ended
Question: What kind of ice cream would you like to have?
Answer: I would like to have a peanut butter and fudge sundae.

Open-ended questions invite a person to share their opinions and feelings, and are critical to effective communication. The ability to ask these types of open-ended questions is equally important when navigating situations in which it's tempting to give advice.

Have you ever noticed that telling someone what to do isn't nearly as effective as when they arrive at the "ah-ha" themselves?

As a mentor, you will inevitably face times when you'll be presented with a challenging situation or a request for advice. Sometimes a mentee will want you to solve her problems for her! Sometimes, you'd rather be the solution to her problem, instead of walking through the painful steps of her figuring it out for herself. However, your solution isn't always the right solution. Often, there is much to be gained in the "learning by experience" process.

The greatest gift a mentor can give is the companionship of life, not all the right answers.

When someone comes to you with a problem to solve or for advice on a challenging situation, abiding by life coaching principles will enable you to step into the role of companion, rather than feeling like a savior who needs to have all the answers. These five simple steps will help you do just that.

Life Coaching Tips for Effective Communication

1. *Listen to their question and story carefully!*
   Don't make assumptions or jump to conclusions. Rather stay curious and listen to what they are saying, and sometimes, what they are not saying.

2. *Restate what you hear!*
   Make sure you're on the same page by clarifying what they have said through restating what you heard. This is a great way to help them feel heard and engaged!

3. *Shape your response with questions!*
   Avoid responding with advice or solutions. Instead, use your discernment and experience to shape questions that will enable them to consider their solution from a fresh perspective.

4. *Encourage a strength!*

   Look for a character strength you see in them that would build their confidence. This also helps guard you from jumping into fix-it mode as you focus on their abilities and God-given strengths.

5. *Ask for permission to share!*

   This isn't about you, so keep the focus on them. If you have a story relevant to their experience, ask for permission before you share it. This guards you from becoming a run-away-story train, derailing from their growth and putting the focus on you. Asking permission to share your story puts the mentee in a teachable position, since they have to agree to listen to you.

While this process may feel awkward, you will be amazed at how effectively it works. When a person feels as though she came up with an answer to her problem or situation, she is much more likely to embrace the solution.

There is nothing like discovering you don't have to have all the answers! By applying life coaching principles in my own mentoring relationships (and especially in my parenting), I've witnessed how the door to serve on my knees—seeking the Lord for His wisdom— has positioned me to be of greater help to those I deeply care for and long to impact.

Reflection Questions

1. How do you feel when someone takes time to notice you? How are you encouraged by a comment or action that responds to how

you are doing personally?

2. In what ways have you been hurt by the lack of noticing happening in your life? Pray about this and consider how you should respond.

3. Do you sometimes feel uncertain how to respond to someone else's problems? Take time now to ask God to give you the ability to listen well and pray it up, instead of feeling compelled to fix everything.

Impact Challenge

Are you sensitive to listening beyond someone's words to decode the story of the heart? If not, try practicing this skill on friends and family, looking beyond the words to hearing what exactly they are hiding or holding within. Then put into practice the five life coaching tips for effective communication.

12

Training

ON THE GO AND IN THE WORD

The "T" in "mentor" stands for *training*, and it incorporates both the practical aspect of teaching the Word and also going beyond in training a mentee in life skills. It's putting into action the principles of Titus 2:3-5, where the goal is to impart a biblical foundation and perspective not only in terms of understanding solid theology, but also in biblical life application.

As we think about the ways to train our mentees, it's incredibly valuable to not only consider the "what" in terms of content and focus, but also the "how." What do I mean by that? Well, consider the different ways you like to take in and process information. If someone gives you a verbal instruction, do you find yourself needing to write it down to remember it? If you read a powerful passage in a book, do you retain it without effort, or must you rewrite it to make it sink in? Can you recall what you see rather easily, like who was wearing what at the last Bible study gathering? The way you process information is reflective of your unique, God-given learning style. Yes, as unique as your personality and spiritual gifting. It all comes together to make you a distinctly wonderful and marvelously unique package

(Psalm 139).

In the same way every thumbprint is unique, no two people are wired exactly the same way.

So as we consider this matter of training our mentee in the ways of God, it's so incredibly important to realize that the way we do things may take on an entirely different approach from the one we're investing in. For example, how we go about imparting a skill, such as cooking or unpacking a Scripture passage, may not work the same way for each of you. That's why understanding each other's spiritual gifting and temperament is as valuable as considering learning styles, or as we call them in the Highlands Ability Battery (HAB), learning channels.

The traditional learning styles are distinguished as auditory (learning by hearing), visual (learning by seeing), and kinesthetic (learning by doing). The following two assessments are useful for gaining quick insight:

- How to Learn: http://www.howtolearn.com/learning-styles-quiz
- Edutopia: http://www.edutopia.org/multiple-intelligences-learning-styles-quiz

If you really want to unpack the way you process information, the HAB will give you insights into your driving abilities (problem solving) as well as learning channels by looking at the following abilities:

Driving Abilities
- Classification: indicates your ability to see relationships between seemingly unrelated events, situations, or informa-

tion. It shows your ability to move from the specific to the general when solving problems. High range indicates great in emergency situations, a quick decision maker.

- Concept Organization: indicates your ability to arrange ideas, information, or things in a logical order. It shows your ability to move from the general to the specific to solve problems and to communicate the logic in doing so.
- Idea Productivity: measures the number of new ideas you can generate within a given time in response to a given stimulus. It does not reflect the quality or creativity of the ideas. It is a measure of the volume or flow of your ideas.
- Spatial Relations Theory (SRT): indicates your ability to see the theoretical relationships that exist in the working of the mechanical universe. It is the ability to understand how systems work, which applies to mechanical systems and interpersonal systems.
- Spatial Relations Visualization (SRV): indicates your ability to see in three dimensions when shown only two. Spatial Relations Visualization is also related to needing hands-on experience and work.

Specialized Abilities

- Design (Image): recall an overall pattern or picture presented in two dimensions, such as a chart, diagram, sketch, and patterns of any kind.
- Observation: pay close attention to visual details, to perceive and remember small changes, and to notice irregularities.
- Verbal (Reading): learn new words and quickly and easily recall what you have read.
- Tonal (Listening): remember what you hear, including tunes and tonal sequences.

- Rhythm (Kinesthetic): remember rhythm patterns, and learning through movement.
- Pitch Discrimination: ability to distinguish fine differences in pitch as well as perceptual discrimination across the senses.
- Number: ability to recall miscellaneous facts and data, which indicate an ability to use numerical information to solve problems and make decisions.
- Visual Speed and Accuracy: ability to read and interpret written symbols quickly and accurately.
- Vocabulary: indicates the verbal level at which you communicate ideas to others; midrange is college educated.

Even if you don't take the HAB, I bet you can pick up on some of the ways you process information and how your distinct learning channels play into your relationships. Imagine now what that looks like in those you want to mentor.

Appreciating each other's God-given wiring is a powerful way of cultivating life-giving relationships.

So let me ask you a critical question: Wouldn't you agree that more important than the "what" of your time together as mentor to mentee, is the "how"—as in the way you're interacting with each other? The training you desire to impart may be focused on godly principles for developing real life skills or Scripture principles for growing deep in solid theological understanding. But in either regard, the approach you take to connecting is as important as the task at hand.

Training Opportunities

Whether as a mom to daughter, aunt to niece, or older friend to younger, the opportunities to mentor in a training capacity are end-less and often spontaneous. It might look like an intentional coffee date conversation with a laptop open as you discuss how to manage a budget or a Saturday afternoon toiling the ground to prepare for a vegetable garden. In that side-by-side time, it may not feel like bibli-cal mentoring, but in the "doing" there is opportunity for training and teaching as Deuteronomy 6 describes. We've considered that passage already, but let's take a closer look:

> Deuteronomy 6:6-9 (MSG)
> *Write these commandments that*
> *I've given you today on your hearts.*
> *Get them inside of you and*
> *then get them inside your children.*
> *Talk about them wherever you are,*
> *sitting at home or walking in the street;*
> *talk about them from the time*
> *you get up in the morning to*
> *when you fall into bed at night.*

Can you see the framework for biblical mentoring in this passage? It's so simple that you might have missed it!

Talking about the Scriptures while doing life side by side is what biblical mentoring is all about.

The training happens naturally, purposefully, organically. Can you see why it's a perfect setting to mentor your own children while they are in your home, since they are accessible? When my oldest daugh-ter was in sixth grade, I had the opportunity to homeschool her for that one year. Instead of focusing on only her academics, I capital-ized on the time we had together to train her up in every aspect of caring for home and family. She learned how to plan a holiday meal, set up a guest room, organize a cupboard, make her own cleaning supplies, plan a budget, and cultivate a quiet time routine. It was Titus 2 in overdrive! If only our circumstances would have allowed for such intentional mentoring for all our children, but alas, that was not God's plan. So with my other girls, and at times my son, I seize the moment to mentor and impart to them these principles of stewardship from a biblical perspective.

Mentoring isn't a one-size fits all endeavor.

While mentoring between moms and their girls, and at times their sons, is an ideal scenario, that's not the only way it should take place. As we've considered already, within the family of God, spiritual mothers are needed in so many ways to fulfill this role of doing life side by side while teaching the commands of God. It's the blood of Christ that connects us, not always our DNA!

The way you spend your time together isn't nearly as important as your heart invested in each other.

So let's consider the organic training opportunities you might be able to embrace, either by reaching out as the older woman or seeking mentoring as the younger woman:

- Planting a garden.
- Cleaning out an over-packed basement.
- Planning a party.
- Preparing for guests.
- Learning how to manage a budget.
- Making meals for thirty days in a one-day cookfest.
- Walking together weekly.

- Serving as a mother's helper to a momma of littles.
- Academic tutoring.
- Teaching a musical instrument.
- Working on a craft together.

While none of these activities seem spiritual, each one lays the backdrop for connecting, sharing, and discussing the Word that God has laid on your heart at that moment. Can you see why following Christ and daily investing time in the Word for yourself is so important in a mentoring relationship?

The Word needs to be in you to flow out of you—and that takes a devotion of time.

If cultivating a rich time in the Word is a struggle for you, take heart. We'll consider creative ways to spark your faith alive and find the time you need in Part 4.

Traditional Teaching Opportunities

An aspect to training is most definitely teaching, and that can certainly take on a more traditional format through making time to study the Scriptures together. That may look like doing a Bible study, using an inductive study method like what's taught by Kay Arthur and Precept Ministries (http://precept.org/about_inductive_bible_study). You might also choose to read a Christian book together, based on something that appeals to both of you or choosing something that focuses on your mentee's age and stage, such as:

For Women of All Ages

- *Sermon on the Mount,* Jen Wilkin

- *Lord, Teach Me to Pray in 28 Days,* Kay Arthur
- *Breaking Free,* Beth Moore
- *Praying God's Word,* Beth Moore
- *Get Out of That Pit,* Beth Moore
- *Disciplines of the Beautiful Woman,* Anne Ortlund
- *Discerning the Voice of God: How to Recognize When God Speaks,* Priscilla Shirer
- *Grace for the Good Girl: Letting Go of the Try-Hard Life,* Emily P. Freeman
- *Meet the New You: A 21-Day Plan for Embracing Fresh Attitudes and Focused Habits for Real Life Change,* Elisa Pulliam
- For a complete list, visit http://www.moretobe.com/2016/06/books-bible-studies-women/

For Tween and Teen Girls (available at moretobe.com)

- *Journey to Freedom: Bible Study on Identity*
- *Mosaic: Bible Study on Life Purpose*
- *Tiny Little Bible Study for Tweens: Cupcake Style*
- *Tiny Little Bible Study for Tweens: Pizza Party*
- Check out a complete list of resources at http://www.more-tobe.com/books-studies-for-teens/

Sharing the Word, while teaching practical life lessons, is at the heart of biblical mentoring along with being intentional about studying the Scriptures together. Whichever way the Lord leads you to cultivate a mentoring relationship, may you embrace it with all the grace He has to offer you.

Reflection Questions

1. What are some of the practical skills you could pass onto a mentee? Consider what skills are unique to your personality and upbringing, lifestyle habits, or experiences, which you could focus on teaching to others.

2. What area of life would you like to receive teaching in? Spend time today looking for those resources and opportunities.

3. What inspires you to want to invest a portion of yourself in others?

13

Offering

TIME AND TALENTS

The "O" in "mentor" stands for *offering*, but maybe not quite in the way think. What is the first thought that comes to mind when you hear the word "offering?" If you've been raised in a church, maybe you hear the cha-ching of a child's pocket change hitting the offering plate. Or, maybe you recall the passage from Malachi 3:10 about bringing your tithes to the storehouses or the New Testament story about the widow putting in the offering box all she had to give.

> Luke 21:1-4 (NKJV)
> *And He looked up and saw the rich putting their gifts into the treasury, and He saw also a certain poor widow putting in two mites. So He said, "Truly I say to you that this poor widow has put in more than all; for all these out of their abundance have put in offerings for God, but she out of her poverty put in all the livelihood that she had."*

She gave out of her poverty. Do we even know what this means? Are we like the rich, giving out of our abundance? Both are good questions worthy of deep reflection when it comes to our financial giving.

They are also worth considering in terms of how we're stewarding our time and talents for the advancing of the kingdom of God, especially as mentors.

We live in a society that focuses so much on building our own storehouses and serving our own needs. Wouldn't you agree that it's counter-cultural to be uncomfortable and stretched in our giving, of any kind? I look at our financial budget and wonder how we'll make ends met, especially as one bill piles up on top of another. Before we bought our house, we went through a step-by-step budgeting process to ascertain our expenses in light of our income. We overestimated for every category with the desire to not be stretched too thin, and yet all our planning couldn't account for the unexpected. The roofing bill came in $3,000 higher than we were told it would be. The boiler needed to be replaced three months later, at the tune of $10,000. Our family suffered three concussions in six months and an ankle injury, adding up to thousands of dollars in medical expenses. And then, the real shocker was finding out that adding a teen driver to our auto insurance policy would more than double our premium. As much as we would like to give out of abundance, it certainly feels like we're being stretched to give out of a lack thereof. And yet, God doesn't call us to give because we have.

He invites us to give with what little we do have—not only in our finances but in every area of life.

He doesn't look for the credential PhD in mentoring to fill the role of impacting another life. He is not searching the land for a woman whose stuff is all together lovely to speak into the lives of the next generation. He's not waiting for our checkbooks or cupboards to be tidied up perfectly, so we feel comfortable giving of ourselves to others. He's simply inviting us to give out of our poverty ... of spirit, finances, time, talents, and even confidence. So what would it look like for your offering before God to be less than perfect? What ways is He inviting you to join Him in His work, especially in mentoring, even though you feel less than prepared? What ways are you resisting His invitation? And what gifts and talents has He poured into you that you can overflow onto others?

Honestly, I struggle to sacrifice my time to meet a need, as I'm often irritated by the disruption in my routine. Ah yes, as I share in *Meet the New You*, I struggle with idolatry of production. My to-do list can easily become my false God. In this area, I have to choose to bring my offering forward, rather than feeling like it's a natural overflow of my giftings. Wouldn't you agree it's much easier to offer out of abundance—as in the ways we feel qualified and agreeable when it comes to serving and responding to needs? But isn't that the rub about our giving, financially or otherwise, as it's all about motive! Is our offering a begrudgingly difficult task that we feel compelled to do by some falsely erected standard or is it a spiritual act of worship?

Romans 12:1
And so, dear brothers and sisters, I plead with you to give your bodies to God because of all he has done for you. Let them be a living and holy sacrifice—the kind he will find acceptable. This is truly the way to worship him.

When our offering is done with pure motives, it becomes a living sacrifice that is truly unadulterated worship. It is about a daily discipline of using our God-given gifts, talents, experiences, and resources to praise God and serve Him in the moment, not only while singing worship songs in church on Sunday mornings.

Talents like ...

- homekeeping
- cooking
- financial planning and bookkeeping
- carpentry and mechanical skills
- artistic abilities, like painting or drawing
- being able to sing or play an instrument
- a computer or technology skill

Experiences like ...

- accomplishing success in business or ministry
- launching a nonprofit
- running a conference
- training volunteers at a community center
- organizing a space
- working with children, teens, or the elderly
- caring for aging parents
- raising special-needs children
- overcoming a broken marriage

Resources like ...

- a home for gathering
- a guest room for extended stays
- an outdoor space for recreation
- a grown-up toy like a boat or motorhome
- generously giving to support a family in need or a missionary

To live with this mindset of offering our time, talents, and resources as our spiritual act of worship is a beautiful thing, but it's not always easy. It requires turning our eyes and ears toward the Lord, and tuning our minds and hearts toward the Holy Spirit's promptings. It is the choice to give thanks and praise, instead of complaining when an inconvenient opportunity arises to serve. It's about putting off and placing on hold your plans, while pushing ahead in a difficult relationship. It's about laying down your agenda for the sake of meeting a real need in someone else's life.

Yes, the offering of biblical mentoring isn't always glamorous. It can be downright uncomfortable. But we haven't been called to comfort. We're called to be the love of Christ to each other, and that requires love in action and not only feelings (1 Corinthians 13).

We're called to move beyond ourselves, our limits, our wants and desires, our expectations and longings as we join God in His work in someone else's life, serving as the hands and feet of Christ.

A Romans 12 life is not one without boundaries or limits. On the contrary, it's a life submitted to God and guided by the Holy Spirit's leading. There will be times in which we'll have to exert a no and pull back from demands. Even Jesus retreated for prayer and time alone with His Father (Matthew 14). There were times in which He served publicly and in which He slipped way.

It's the pure offering that God is after—when the motives of our hearts are right before Him.

Burnout is not part of God's plan. Serving from the overflow of His work in us is, however, as we use the time, talents, and resources He's given us to impact those we're called to mentor.

Reflection Questions

1. Do you find it a challenge to serve others with a good attitude? Why or why not?

2. What do you have to give as a mentor?

3. Is your giving pure? As in, are you doing it for the glory of God, the approval of others, out of a sense of duty, or for your own satisfaction?

Impact Challenge

Seek the Lord on this today, carving out twelve minutes to pray about this one very important biblical principle. Then see if you can write down twelve simple responsibilities in which you could focus on doing with a spiritual act of worship mindset.

14

Responding

BEING "RESPONSE ABLE"

The "R" in "mentor" stands for learning how to be *response able*.
This is a concept I picked up in the life coach course I teach, as we
consider the critical difference between reacting and responding.

For example, we react to a situation when our emotions catch us by
surprise, when our values are compromised, or when we haven't
taken the time to prepare. Of course, reacting is inevitable in a crisis
situation that couldn't have been prevented, like an accident or
medical diagnosis. But how many times have we reacted to a situation simply because we neglected our responsibilities or ignored
the warning signs? It's like knowing that I'll be predictably hungry
at 11:30 am sharp, and not scheduling in time for lunch. My hangry
(hungry plus angry) will take over and I'll react with a short fuse
rather than the patience I desire to have with anyone who crosses my
path. Wouldn't you say that reaction could have been avoided?

So rather than being mentors who react, the goal is to become
women who are "response able." What do I mean by that? Well,
to be "response able" is all about being able to respond rather than

reacting to a situation. In other words, it's the pause before the crisis to closely look at the practical and spiritual needs from two perspectives: ours and the ones we're called to mentor.

Oh yes, self-awareness is a necessary component in mentoring.

In the same way that a nurse checks our vitals at a doctor's visit, we need to be aware of what is going on in our lives so we can respond well to others—not only those we're mentoring, but anyone we're in a relationship with. So, to be "response able," we've got to consider the factors that may stand in our way as we make a commitment to a lifestyle of mentoring. It's like taking a pulse on our spiritual heartbeat through asking honest questions of ourselves and before the Lord, such as:

What is going on with my emotional health?

- Am I bitter?
- Am I unforgiving?
- Am I critical?
- Am I scared?
- Am I worried?
- Am I sad?
- Am I in a fight or conflict with someone?
- Am I mad at someone one?
- Am I in a season of trial or suffering?

What is going on with my spiritual health?

- Am I questioning God?
- Am I mad at God?
- Am I growing in my relationship with God?

- Am I growing in my study of Scripture?
- Am I struggling with a biblical discipline?
- Am I struggling in my church community?
- Am I in accountability relationships with other believers?

What is going on with my physical health?

- Am I worn down?
- Am I having trouble sleeping?
- Am I struggling with an illness or disease?
- Am I battling weight loss/gain?
- Am I injured?
- Am I in need of exercise?
- Am I in need of physical rest?

What is going on overall?

- What do I find myself thinking about all the time?
- What unresolved issues need attention?
- What feels like an obstacle in my life today?
- How is that obstacle impacting the way I feel?
- How am I spending my time?
- How am I spending my resources?
- What area of life needs the most focus right now?

Becoming aware of what is going on in our hearts and minds enables us to respond appropriately and authentically.

While we don't have to spill the beans about everything going on in our lives, we don't have to hide the distractions and trials either—that's only possible, however, if we've owned where we are at. A simple, honest explanation (lacking in detail) can draw you closer together rather than separating you by the "elephant in the room." Consider this type of response: "Hey, I'm really struggling with some health issues right now that are keeping me from operating at 100 percent. I'd love to meet with you every week, but how about we meet face to face one week a month and over the phone the other weeks?" Is that better than pretending you don't have limitations or making excuses that don't add up? Being self-aware and honest about the state of our lives is the only way to fight against the guilt of not being enough, while carving out grace space to offer exactly what we have to give.

I love to come back to Colossians 3 (you'll notice I quote it often), as it lays such a grace-filled format for living a life of responding instead of reacting. Paul calls us to be aware of that old self and put on the clothing of the new self.

Colossians 3:10
Put on your new nature, and be renewed as you learn to know your Creator and become like him.

Wouldn't you agree that while God gets mad, He doesn't get even? He is sad, but not manipulative. He is grieved, but not overcome with a critical and bitter spirit. He feels, but chooses to respond instead of react.

God is "response able."

What does it look like to follow His example, so that the message of Christ comes through loud and clear to those we choose to mentor?

Colossians 3:12-17
Since God chose you to be the holy people he loves, you must clothe yourselves with tenderhearted mercy, kindness, humil-

ity, gentleness, and patience. Make allowance for each other's faults, and forgive anyone who offends you. Remember, the Lord forgave you, so you must forgive others. Above all, clothe yourselves with love, which binds us all together in perfect harmony. And let the peace that comes from Christ rule in your hearts. For as members of one body you are called to live in peace. And always be thankful.

Let the message about Christ, in all its richness, fill your lives. Teach and counsel each other with all the wisdom He gives. Sing psalms and hymns and spiritual songs to God with thankful hearts. And whatever you do or say, do it as a representative of the Lord Jesus, giving thanks through Him to God the Father.

It's a choice to put on tenderhearted mercy, kindness, humility, gentleness, and patience. It's a choice to make allowances for each other's faults and to forgive offenses. It's a choice to love and pursue harmony and unity. It's a choice to let the peace of Christ dwell in us. It's a choice to be thankful. It's our choice in how we'll live and teach, counsel and train up those we mentor! But that choice is not made without His wisdom. We get to come under the teaching and leading of the Holy Spirit as we seek to respond to those we mentor. We are more than just cheerleaders and teachers, encouragers and companions. We are also accountability partners, so we need to have our stuff in order before calling them out on theirs!

Yes, responding to her needs and circumstances is a heavy responsibility. At times, she will need hope spoken and love given. Other times will require a gentle rebuke and kick in the pants, especially when she's headed down the wrong road. As Jesus teaches in Matthew 7, we want to help our mentees choose the narrow road for their life journey, and to stay off the broad road that leads to destruction.

Matthew 7:13-14 (ESV)
Enter by the narrow gate. For the gate is wide and the way is easy that leads to destruction, and those who enter by it are many. For the gate is narrow and the way is hard that leads to life, and those who find it are few.

As mentors, we have the opportunity to stand at that wide gate and shout, "Turn! Don't go this way! Please heed this instruction!" Yes, we can share our stories and offer our wisdom, bathed in prayer and washed with the Word. We can beckon and encourage our mentee to position herself on the narrow road that leads to life. We can point out that small gate and encourage that step of faith toward a better future. The Scriptures say only a few find the narrow gate. Is that because it takes a careful eye to see it? Possibly. Or maybe that is because it also requires a more determined step?

At each turn of your mentee's life, she will have a choice to make. As you journey with her, your goal is to offer your wisdom, experience, and biblical truth to help her navigate her course. You stand at the crossroads waiting for her, doing all the things a mentor does (meeting, encouraging, noticing, teaching, offering), but with open hands raised toward the cross and an overflowing amount of grace.

2 Corinthians 12:9 (NIV)
But He said to me, "My grace is sufficient for you, for my power is made perfect in weakness." Therefore I will boast all the more gladly about my weaknesses, so that Christ's power may rest on me.

For a mentoring relationship to grow in spiritual maturity, both together and individually, grace is a necessary ingredient.

Grace says I'm not sufficient for your needs, but I know the One who is.

As you are stretched beyond your human ability, grace will enable you to let the relationship take its God-ordained course, trusting His perfect plan. You can't make her walk through the narrow gate. She needs to decide for herself and you need to give her permission to do so. If she ends up on the wrong path, you can be the one she runs to when she decides to turn the other way ... ready to put her life right into Jesus' arms.

You get to offer her unwavering love, even while she challenges authority and manipulates emotions. That's why being prayed up is so critical. The words that come from your mouth need to be in response to her actions, not reacting to them—God can order your words when you yield your heart and mind to Him.

The Word promises that truth spoken in love is the source of growth, so seize opportunities to respond to your mentee's life in the pleasant times with an outpouring of Scripture training. When you return to the Word during difficult times, it will be less of a shock and more of a comfort to her, because of the foundation of Scripture already established in her life and your relationship. Ask the Lord for His Spirit to lead you and strengthen you as you invest tangibly in her spiritual growth.

Reflection Questions

1. What is your tendency? To react? To respond? And why?

2. How do you feel about becoming more self-aware? What areas
    of strain, stress, or weakness do you need to be cognizant of?

3. How can you prepare yourself to respond to a mentee's needs
    both in the good times and difficult ones?

PART FOUR

Make an Impact

*"Though we certainly need each other,
no one but God is indispensable."*

Dr. Henry Cloud and Dr. John Townsend

*Boundaries: When to Say YES and When to
Say NO to Take Control of Your Life*

15

Deeply Rooted

Do you feel like you're drinking from a fire hose after considering the six steps of mentoring? Well, then imagine me tossing you a towel because it's time to dry off your face and take your place in the mentoring race. Yes, let's circle back to the idea of mentoring being like a relay race in which you pass the baton from one generation to the next. This time, however, think of that race in broader terms— as your personal marathon race from here to eternity. It's time to consider how you'll run your personal race of faith so you'll have the endurance and perseverance necessary in cultivating biblical mentoring relationships.

1 Corinthians 9:24
Do you not know that in a race all the runners run, but only one receives the prize? So run that you may obtain it.

Imagine your chest leaning forward, legs pumping hard, as you break the finish line with all you've got left. It's an Eric Lidell moment— running fast and enjoying every moment of the experience. That's because your eye is on the prize of seeing the Lord face to face, knowing you did everything you could to run the race of faith well, determined to give Him all the glory.

From the very beginning of this study, I've emphasized that our faith in Jesus Christ as Lord is the foundation for biblical mentoring. We must follow Christ distinctly if we are to mentor biblically. But what does following Christ "distinctly" really look like?

To follow Christ distinctly simply means to do so clearly and unmistakable. Our words and actions communicate the same message.

We are disciples of Christ, first and foremost. Our faith can't be lip service. It must hang on actions that are often sacrificial and inconvenient. In biblical terms, it looks like devotion and discipline that foster a deeply rooted life in Christ.

> Colossians 2:7 (NLT)
> *Let your roots grow down into him, and let your lives be built on him. Then your faith will grow strong in the truth you were taught, and you will overflow with thankfulness.*

Do you find yourself resisting the necessary steps for growing a deeply rooted faith? Are you running from legalism? Fear of failure? Or maybe your rebellious nature just doesn't want to be told what to do. I get it. But that doesn't make it right. We can get around the fact that to cultivate a rich relationship with God, one that is deeply rooted and overflowing with His presence, we need to actually spend time with Him getting to know His character, promises, and commands on a daily basis.

A deeply rooted faith grows through studying the Word, spending time in prayer, and being invested in iron-sharpening-iron relationships within the body of Christ.

Yet, would you agree that our lives often feel too busy to make
this kind of daily investment of our time? We have practical needs
demanding our attention every day. Who's going to fold the laundry?
Pay the bills? Get the family where they have to go? Who's going to
do our homework? Serve at church on Sunday morning? Finish our
last task at work before rushing home? It often feels like the buck
stops right here, with you and me, doesn't it? How do we put off any
of those necessary things in order to make time for our relationship
with God?

Hmm, doesn't that question sound a little bit like the enemy's whisper telling us it isn't possible? So let me ask you, are we being duped
by lies from the pit of hell, tempting us to believe that we simply
don't have the time to invest in our relationship with the Lord? That
if we even try, we risk not getting everything else done and disap-
pointing our family and friends?

I must confess I have struggled to put off the tyranny of the urgent to
devote time to God too many days of my Christian walk. Have you
felt this too? Maybe you've even prayed like me,

> *Heavenly Father, I give you this day. Please order it according to*
> *Your purposes and show me Your work that I might join You in it.*

And then run off to do what you thought needed to be done until
another nudge comes your way, *Read your Bible, too. Don't skip this*
step.

A deep sigh. I know. Why do we resist this precious invitation to
spend time with God in His Word? Oh sure, I've been "Super Bible
Woman" plenty of times, abandoning the dishes in the sink while
I've lunged into my Bible study homework, not caring who walked
into the house. But those times seem to mark the desperate years,

when time in the Word was like air for me to breathe. Fortunately, desperate hasn't been my normal, but that also means time with the Lord is something I have to be disciplined about. Is it this way for you too? Or are you tempted by something else, like watching a TV show, sleeping a little later, shopping a little longer?

I suppose if we looked closely at the pattern of our devotion to the Lord, it would clearly coincide with the rhythms and trials of our lives. When life falls apart ... ahem ... cancer, injuries, depression, rejection, loneliness, divorce, division ... we run to God. At first. But when we feel like He doesn't answer, we might run away. We might push Him away. We might just go numb.

Temperamental Faith

My faith is as temperamental as my personality, but by God's grace, He's convicted me that my faith ought not to be based on feelings. Neither should yours.

To grow into women who mentor biblically, we need to meet with the Lord daily.

There, I said it. If we are going to follow Christ distinctly, we need to do more than know of Christ, we need to spend time with Him personally. We need to read the Word, lingering long enough to allow the Holy Spirit time to teach and guide us in all truth (John 15:26).

We simply must develop the discipline of making time for God and digging deep into His Word, as that's the only way we'll be filled up to overflowing and able to sustain the investment we long to offer in the mentoring relationships God brings into our lives. So what does that practically look like? Consider these simple and practical steps:

Evaluate Your Time

Take the time to look at your life and evaluate your schedule (download free time evaluation resources from elisapulliam. com). Decide on a realistic approach for spending your time with the Lord and in the Word. Maybe this isn't the season in which you should do an inductive Bible study, but maybe you can make time to read a chapter of the Bible a day on your smart phone.

Embark on a Realistic Plan

Make a short term plan for how you are going to devote time to being with the Lord and in His word each week. Decide on a time, place, and what you'll do for your quiet time routine. The Starting Point Method described in *Meet the New You: A 21-Day for Embracing Fresh Attitudes and Focused Habits for Real Life Change* could be a great way for you to get started. You might also choose to use the simple Bible Reading Plan described on the blog at *More to Be*: http://www.moretobe.com/2016/05/week-4-meet-new-book-club-overcome-obstacles.

Engage Your Heart and Mind

There's never a time when we shouldn't seek out the teaching of seasoned pastors and Bible study leaders, maybe even picking up books theologians would normally study in order to stretch our minds and hearts to the things of God. Yes, being a perpetual student of the Word is a good thing, since as we mature in life and take in new experiences, our understanding of biblical principles will grow in depth and breadth.

Embrace His Grace

Every day will bring new challenges and unexpected situations. It is great to have a plan in place, but embrace God's grace for you when you fall short and stumble. Don't give up, but face each new day with the new mercies God offers you.

Can you think of the many benefits of devoting time to getting to know God through time spent in the Word, especially when it comes to mentoring? How about these, to name a few:

- ability to see the world through a biblical lens
- Scripture to draw upon in crisis
- perspective check in the face of cultural norms
- being able to pray the Word, when words are hard to find
- understanding of God's character, especially when circumstances don't make sense
- promises of hope to cling to in the good times and bad

The more we know of the biblical narrative and the character of God, the more we are shaped by it. As our spiritual roots grow down deep, the fruit of our lives will blossom vibrantly. That's what is seen by those around us, and it becomes a compelling invitation for pursuing God personally. Isn't that what we would hope to happen in those we mentor? It's not "do as I say," but rather, "do as I do."

Our example weighs far more heavily than a lecture.

We might desire for our mentees to grow spiritually and emotionally, but it first starts with us modeling that process. Yes, if we long for their growth, it first starts with ours.

Reflection Questions

1. Who are the people God has put in your life to run the mentoring race with, even if you never considered these relationships from a mentoring perspective before:

   - Those who've come before you?

   - Those alongside you?

   - Those coming after you?

2. What is the state of your relationship with God as of today? Is it vibrant? Weak? Needing a restart?

3. How do you prefer to spend time with God? What does it look like to make that a priority in your life?

16

Technique with Some Tea

If you're anything like me, you've about had it with all the philosophical theorizing about mentoring and are ready to get right into it. Well then, this chapter is for you as we unpack the nitty-gritty of technique and a very practical way of using tea. But before we jump in, let's face the reality of our limits and responsibilities. No matter how much our hearts may be invested in this idea of mentoring, our lives may not have the room needed to jump right in.

Wouldn't you agree that the demands on our time are endless? As I write this, I have over two hundred emails in my inbox awaiting my attention, which are different than the one hundred and seventy-six hanging out there in the first edition of this book—and I still like to keep my inbox empty of anything not pressing. There is no way I'll be able to take care of all those requests, plus respond to the needs of the children and my dear husband, who'd like to have a semiconscious wife to spend time with later this evening. Top that off with a house crying out for a dust bunny war, a ministry website with five pending posts waiting to be approved, and, well, I could go on and on. I bet you can too.

**Life happens. So does biblical mentoring.
Sometimes formally, sometimes casually,
but always with Christ as the focus.**

And so, as we consider stepping forward to put mentoring into action
in our lives, I urge you to do so knowing it will look as unique as
your God-given design in the body of Christ. It will also change dramatically with each season and stage of your life, too. Yet, no matter
when and where mentoring happens, there are two key how-tos that
are timeless and effective at keeping Christ in the center of your
mentoring relationships: The Three Story Technique and tea—yes, as
in the kind you sip and savor.

The Three-Story Technique

I always had a heart for encouraging younger girls and sharing lessons of life with them. Even as far back as high school, I would take
a few younger friends under my wing. Once I became a Christian in
college, and returned home, I settled into a local church and began
working with the youth ministry. Two years later my husband and I
found ourselves living with forty teenage boys at a boarding school,
which made me pretty desperate for spending time with girls of any
age. I jumped at the opportunity to serve in the girls' dorm one night
a week to "officially" supervise study hours while seizing opportunities to informally mentor.

Some of these girls came from broken homes and reckless relationships, full of fear about their futures. Others came from well-caring
families, but had real concerns about what life would be like in
college and beyond. Both kinds were eager to hear about the life of
a newly married twenty-something, and were happy to do anything
but study or clean their rooms, and so we often passed the between

study hours and lights out to connect heart to heart. I found myself sharing stories as a way of answering their life-questions, rather than lecturing on a particular biblical principle. By giving them snapshots of my life nestled between the truths found in Scripture, God opened the doors to their heart.

In the same way Jesus uses parables in the Scriptures to illustrate God's instructions, what I shared painted a picture of God's work in my life. My stories were really a retelling of Christ's stories that had been written in my heart.

> 2 Corinthians 3:3
> *Clearly, you are a letter from Christ showing the result of our ministry among you. This "letter" is written not with pen and ink, but with the Spirit of the living God. It is carved not on tablets of stone, but on human hearts.*

While my testimony has often been the foundation of my storytelling and the launching point of my mentoring relationships, it doesn't end there.

As we walk with the Lord, our testimony becomes greater than our salvation story.

Each lesson of faith we learn along the way is a lesson to pass on to the next generation. Each act of God's grace that has transformed our lives is an act to proclaim. Each moment of sin overcome by repentance is one to brag on God about. Stories set the backdrop for mentoring relationships as they draw us together and provide a framework for teachable moments. Often, my Evening Tea & Chat (ETC)gatherings begin with a prayed-up, thought-through, Holy Spirit-led story relevant to the topic. It is amazing to watch the Lord use my real-life fumbles and foibles to touch the hearts of a dozen or so teenage girls filling my living room.

Honesty and humility are both compelling teachers.

Curious minds are hungry for truth, but the pathway to their hearts comes through story. They want to be taught, but not lectured. So I share an experience. I reveal a struggle. I confess a lesson learned. I allude to a sin, without the gory details, but to get their attention. They are unforced discipleship moments, when we find ourselves connecting heart to heart, not only back in my days at the boarding school, but any place we can connect in conversation. With teenagers in my home, it often happens while digging spoons into a gallon of ice cream together. It may also happen through a phone conversation with a college gal or in the corners of church after Bible study. These story-giving times fold into everyday life and become as much a part of my mentoring as they are a part of my parenting.

Real life offers the potential to illustrate biblical principles in ways that a sermon or study alone may not always accomplish. From each story, I stroll into the Truth, tying the lesson together with a biblical principle and verses to support the application. This pattern is really what the Three Story Technique is all about. It's a three-fold approach for cultivating rich mentoring relationships through pointing to the God-story in each other's lives.

Story 1: Your Story

What about your life circumstances and relationships—past and present—reveal God's hand and valuable lessons learned? What about your hopes for the future convey a side of God's design in how He made you? What attribute(s) of God have you experienced personally and can share about with passion?

Story 2: Their Story

How has God orchestrated the details of your mentees' lives? What is unique about His design in their personalities, gifting, experiences? What do they believe about themselves, God, and others? How is His purpose unfolding in their lives today?

Story 3: His Story

The most important story to discover is the one about Jesus Christ. By knowing the gospel message and the breadth of Scripture, take both of your stories to see them through the lens of His story, which matters most of all.

The Three Story Technique is a way to approach mentoring relationships from a position of curiosity rather than presumption. It leaves room for you to see what God is doing and join Him in it. Because it is really about Him and THEM! As members within the body of Christ, we each have a particular role to fill, unique to our gifts, talents, and experiences—this is our part of the story in HIStory!

The way we mentor will be entirely unique to the stories we tell. They come from the lessons we've learned, the lives we've lived, and the Christ we love. When used for the glory of God and His purposes, our stories are a powerful tool in impacting others with an eternal perspective.

Pour a Cup of Tea

As simple as it may seem, the most practical thing you can do to set the tone for your mentoring relationships is to fix yourself a tea basket and have it on hand at a moment's notice. Grab a wicker basket from the dollar store, select half a dozen boxes of tea on sale at the local supermarket, discard the boxes, and fill your basket to overflowing. Keep it stocked and even in sight. Why? Because tea can remind us of "t," and that little "t" can remind of us the cross.

The cross is the symbol of our faith because it is where our relationship with God becomes a reality and our new birth in Christ a possibility. It's where Jesus conquered death and rose again, and it's a perfect reminder to us that Jesus is the only Savior anyone ever needs.

The people you love don't need you as much as they need Jesus.

You simply need to live each moment, humbly and boldly giving off the aroma of Christ because of your deep, authentic, and life-transforming personal relationship with your Redeemer (2 Corinthians 2:15).

While serving tea may be the key to cultivating a warm and inviting setting for your mentees to open up, it is truly the cross that holds the key to their heart and opens the door for them to experience life transformed. So if Jesus (and His work on the cross) is to be the foundation of our mentoring relationships, then why not incorporate a simple little reminder into our technique?

If you think about it, a hot cup of tea also makes us slow down. The water has to boil. The tea has to steep. Then it has to cool enough to drink it. Tea makes time stop and forces us to savor the moment. And while your tea is brewing, there's a window of time for chatting. Of course, if you don't like tea, sneak in some hot chocolate packets and even a few special instant coffee treats.

Having a tea basket on hand also makes hosting an ETC gathering super easy. In preparation for each meeting time, all you have to do is boil some water, grab a stack of mugs, and position them on the kitchen counter with the tea basket. This little touch of hospitality is a cinch to have on hand and prepared ahead of time, so you won't be distracted from onnecting with your guests when they arrive.

I promised to give you mentoring simplified, didn't I? And I honestly believe that embracing this idea of not forgetting the tea will enable you to move forward with confidence in your mentoring journey. So, how about fixing your tea basket right now?

Reflection Questions

1. What do you believe about yourself in light of God's design of you and your life?

2. What do you believe about God's sovereignty and goodness?

3. What is it about your life circumstances and relationships—past and present—and your hopes for the future, that make you unique?

4. What do you think about assembling a tea basket? If this doesn't resonate with you, what could you do to prepare your heart for cross-centered hospitality?

17

Impact Life

Sometimes, we can get so caught up in a method that we complicate the process of actually moving forward in our mission. So how about you sit back and take a deep breath as we wrap up this study by getting back to the basics. Take a minute to think about this question:

Why is mentoring important to you?

Forget everything you've learned thus far. Just reflect on what drew you into this deeper study about mentoring. Were you looking for a way to improve your mentoring skills? Did you want to figure out how to find a mentor? Were you hoping to uncover some secret sauce that would make your mentoring relationships feel more successful? Were you just curious about mentoring, in general? There's all sorts of reasons why this topic of mentoring is important to you, but let me be crass for a moment: So what! Wouldn't you agree that it's one thing for it to be important to you, but another thing altogether to do something about it?

What you're passionate about doesn't change the world in the same way as joining God in the work He has called you to.

Learning more about a topic isn't going to make any difference unless you act upon what you've learned. So, let me ask you this: What are you going to do with what you've learned about mentoring? We covered a lot of ground in this journey of discovering what it means to mentor biblically! By now, you're well acquainted with your excuses and have discovered how to trump them with the truth! I also hope you're seeing your story in light of His story and have gained fresh vision for joining God in His work. But again, "So what!" How will you take what you've discovered and put it into action?

Maybe you're not yet sure what to do, and that's okay. But it doesn't mean you do nothing. On the contrary, you take the most important next step: Wait on God in prayer! Press into your relationship with Him and focus on growing those faith roots down deep, while asking Him to give you eyes to see the ways He wants to use your time and talents and resources as a mentor.

Hebrews 12:2
We do this by keeping our eyes on Jesus, the champion who initiates and perfects our faith.

Friend, simply bow down before the cross and position yourself to hear from God. He'll lead you, guide you, and equip you in this mentoring journey.

Ephesians 3:14-21 (MSG)
My response is to get down on my knees before the Father, this magnificent Father who parcels out all heaven and earth. I ask him to strengthen you by his Spirit—not a brute strength but a glorious inner strength—that Christ will live in you as you open the door and invite him in. And I ask him that with both feet planted firmly on love, you'll be able to take in with all followers of Jesus the extravagant dimensions of Christ's love. Reach out

and experience the breadth! Test its length! Plumb the depths!
Rise to the heights! Live full lives, full in the fullness of God.

God will do far more than you could ever ask or imagine!

While you wait to see what God will do, I pray you think about who He wants you to serve, right here and right now. Mentoring will happen whether you choose to be intentional about it through using a group format or casually coming alongside a mentee. Simply doing real life together requires real relationships, right? But imagine if those relationships took on a whole new perspective!

Let me paint the picture of how real life mentoring looks in my life. Consider this as a pattern, not a formula, and then prayerfully pursue God's heart for how mentoring could look for you.

Children and Family

I consider myself a mentor to my children first and foremost. If I'm not mentoring them in a way that will leave a lasting impact, who will? So I use the six steps of mentoring as an evaluation tool for the way I engage with my children. For example, I might ask myself, "When was the last time I intentionally listened to Leah? Did I encourage Abby when she came to me last night? Was I 'response able' to Kaitlyn's needs this morning? How am I offering my time to Luke?" But mentoring isn't only for moms! Consider how all the mentoring principles we've learned translate easily into a relationship between an aunt and niece or grandma and granddaughter!

Younger Women and Teen Girls

As I spend time at church or in Bible study, I'm constantly asking God to show me who needs to be encouraged. I ask Him to give me the courage to step out and extend an invitation for coffee, with the desire to simply listen and serve. If I see a younger gal, I'll strive to speak a sincere word of blessing into her life and see where it leads. Occasionally, a formal mentoring relationship might emerge. With the teens I've mentored over the years, it's come through a natural connection established through my daughter's friends or common community, and our mentoring relationships are often cultivated through interactions in my home or text messages.

Groups and Gatherings

I love the way mentoring can take place in a group setting using the ETC format (learn more at moretobe.com/etc/) for gathering a number of girls together in my home for teaching and encouragement. When it comes to noticing and responding, I carefully watch each girl, from the moment she arrives, looking at her body language to discern what is going on in her heart. I seek the Lord throughout this time, asking Him to whisper to my heart about their needs, while actively looking for ways to inspire each of them and enable them to navigate life once they leave my home.

This kind of group mentoring is exhilarating for me, especially when I am blessed with mentoring partners. These sister-mentors may sit quietly during our gathering, but I know they are praying hard. I love to see each one engage according to her own personality and witness the valuable role they play in the one-on-one follow up time.

So, who do you think God is calling you to reach out and mentor? Maybe it looks completely different from my examples. Is God calling you to reach a group of women who have suffered abuse or need post-abortion healing? Is your heart bent toward helping women recover from a broken marriage or the loss of a child? Do you long to help women who need to advance their education or career? Would you like to mentor women in ministry or a particular business role? Your tribe is about your God-given appointment, and that's a by-product of your experiences and wiring. To find your people, look at your soapbox passion—you know, that issue or need you feel compelled to do something about. Those are the people God may be calling you to come alongside as a biblical mentor. That's the race He's asking you to run, and while it may not be clear at the moment, it will be in time. Quite possibly, your mentoring race is just beginning.

1 Corinthians 9:24-27 (MSG)
You've all been to the stadium and seen the athletes race. Everyone runs; one wins. Run to win. All good athletes train hard. They do it for a gold medal that tarnishes and fades. You're after one that's gold eternally.

It's time to press into the wind and run hard for the finish line. Let's give it everything we've got and go for the prize of eternal glory—that legacy of impact we long to leave behind. May our determination to follow Christ distinctly and our desire to overflow the fullness of Him onto others be our testimony from this day forward and forevermore.

Let us be known as women who impacted the next generation for the glory of God.

Reflection Questions

1. Now that you've read this to-do list, what steps are you ready to take first? Highlight them or jot them down in a notebook.

2. Next to those steps, indicate tentative dates by which you'd like to accomplish them as well as the name of someone who can hold you accountable.

3. Devote at least five minutes a day toward praying for those the Lord has positioned you to influence. Begin with your family, praying for each person by name, giving thanks to the Lord for their place in your life. Then continue on in your praying to lift up your friends, colleagues, and acquaintances. Ask the Lord to reveal to you how to influence them for Christ. Finally, pray for those you feel God leading you to mentor.

Impact Challenge

As you shift toward being intentional about mentoring, you may want to use a checklist system to stay purposeful and prayerful. Record your thoughts about your mentor and prayer concerns as well as any actions you'd like to take for each of the nine steps.

Meeting: What type of plan will work for you when it comes to mentoring one-on-one?

Encouraging: How can you reach out in both word and deed to bless the younger woman you feel called to mentor?

Noticing: What is going on in your heart and hers?

Training: How can you focus on biblical principles and life application?

Offering: What ways can you offer your time, talents, and resources as your spiritual act of worship?

Responding: What do you need to do so you can be "response able"?

Resources

"She potentially missed out on watching a miracle because she was depending on herself to feed the people ... It isn't me doing the work for God, but it is me trusting God to do the work in me ... Worship, not work, flows out of the hearts of those who believe."

Emily P. Freeman

Grace for the Good Girl

Becoming a Disciple of Christ

From the beginning of time, God has been calling His people to enter into a personal relationship with Him—a relationship built on the foundation of sacrificial love. God is not merely some cosmic force, tossing the stars into the sky and spinning the earth into rotation, casually creating people and turning them loose like a wind-up toy.

**God is holy and perfect,
strong and tender,
merciful and loving.**

He created us in His very image and longs for us to worship Him wholeheartedly in everything we do. As a part of His perfect plan, God desires for us to belong to the family of God as His beloved children. He is prepared to bestow on us this priceless gift of salvation and the richness of His inheritance, made possible only through faith in Jesus Christ as Lord and Savior.

Ephesians 1:3-13 (ESV)
Blessed be the God and Father of our Lord Jesus Christ, who has blessed us in Christ with every spiritual blessing in the heavenly places, even as he chose us in him before the foundation of the world, that we should be holy and blameless before him. In

love he predestined us for adoption as sons through Jesus Christ,
according to the purpose of his will, to the praise of his glori-
ous grace, with which he has blessed us in the Beloved. In him
we have redemption through his blood, the forgiveness of our
trespasses, according to the riches of his grace, which he lav-
ished upon us, in all wisdom and insight making known to us the
mystery of his will, according to his purpose, which he set forth
in Christ as a plan for the fullness of time, to unite all things
in him, things in heaven and things on earth. In him we have
obtained an inheritance, having been predestined according to
the purpose of him who works all things according to the counsel
of his will, so that we who were the first to hope in Christ might
be to the praise of his glory. In him you also, when you heard the
word of truth, the gospel of your salvation, and believed in him,
were sealed with the promised Holy Spirit, who is the guarantee
of our inheritance until we acquire possession of it, to the praise
of his glory.

God is calling us into a relationship with Him through faith in His Son. The question is how will we respond to this call? Will we ignore it, silence it, or let it go through to spiritual voicemail? Or will we respond to His call and embrace Jesus' sacrifice made on the cross on our behalf?

John 6:65 (ESV)
And he said, "This is why I told you that no one can come to me
unless it is granted him by the Father."

Maybe the reason we hesitate is because we don't feel like we're good enough to hear from God? Maybe we're ashamed about our past mistakes? Maybe we're concerned that we'll never measure up to God's expectations?

It seems most of us can point out our imperfections rather quickly. We know what is wrong with us, even if we're wearing the mask of a perfectly poised woman in all of our social circles and churchy functions.

The truth of the matter is that we'll never be able to get it all together and be good enough for God.

We will always mess up. We will rebel against those in authority over us. Break promises. Betray friends. Burden our lives with thoughts and actions we know are wrong. We're a mess, plain and simple. That's because we are sinners.

> 2 Corinthians 5:20-21 (ESV)
> *Therefore, we are ambassadors for Christ, God making his appeal through us. We implore you on behalf of Christ, be reconciled to God. For our sake he made him to be sin who knew no sin, so that in him we might become the righteousness of God.*

Sin is disobedience against God's will, as revealed through His Word and the working of the Holy Spirit. The Scriptures are full of wonderful instructions on how to live, what to watch out for, what to steer clear from, and how to treat others. But in our desire to be in control (and be our own god), we dismiss God's instruction and head down our own course of destruction. This disobedience erects a wall between us and God, and it also damages our earthly relationships. As we live with pride, bitterness, betrayal, lack of forgiveness, deception, and so on, we grow further and further away from those we love and especially God.

> Ephesians 2:8-9
> *God saved you by his grace when you believed. And you can't take credit for this; it is a gift from God.*

Salvation is not a reward for the good things we have done, so none of us can boast about it.

It may seem utterly incomprehensible, but our merciful creator God allowed His Son, Jesus Christ, to make a way to tear down those walls erected by our sin and open the gates to eternity. When Jesus took the punishment for our sin on the cross, His shed blood became the wrecking ball that knocks down the wall between us and God.

Jesus came to the earth because of God's perfect plan to rescue His people.

He died on the cross, shedding His blood as the only necessary (atoning) sacrifice for our sin. When He rose from the grave, He proved that God's Word was true and that the sacrifice of His death was totally acceptable before God.

As we walk this earth, we will feel the consequences of our sin in our human condition, but we no longer have to live in that mess apart from God. We also have the hope of eternal life, promised only to those who believe in Jesus Christ as Lord.

> John 3:16 (ESV)
> *For God so loved the world, that he gave his only Son, that whoever believes in him should not perish but have eternal life.*

Even though it wasn't His fault, Jesus Christ took upon Himself the burden of our sin because of His love for His Father demonstrated by His obedience to the point of death. So what is expected in return? Simply put, God wants us to tell Him about our sin and our need for a Savior (confession), as we turn from our wrongdoing into right living (repentance). He wants us to receive His forgiveness, grace, and mercy as a sign of His love. Most of all, He wants us to live for His glory and not our own as He offers us a peace and joy that we have never experienced before.

Romans 10:9-10
If you confess with your mouth that Jesus is Lord and believe in your heart that God raised him from the dead, you will be saved. For it is by believing in your heart that you are made right with God, and it is by confessing with your mouth that you are saved.

When we surrender our lives to Christ, He not only tears down the wall between us and God, but He also gives us the Holy Spirit to become our personal guide. And He paves the road to heaven with an overflowing measure of hope, grace, love, mercy, and forgiveness, showing us how to live as sinners saved by grace.

2 Corinthians 5:17
This means that anyone who belongs to Christ has become a new person. The old life is gone; a new life has begun!

God knows we will never be able to make ourselves good enough to be in a relationship with Him, so He gives us Christ to make us right and change us from the inside out. In doing so, He also changes us from the outside in, making us a living testimony for others to witness the power of God at work in a sinner's life. In Christ, we become a new creation and can see life from an eternal perspective— one that brings life purpose into sharp focus as we discover God's unfolding plan. Don't you think that is a better way to live?

Would you like to experience life transformation today?

Apart from faith in Christ as Lord and Savior, our earthly experience is lived without a personal relationship with God, and the outcome is dire. Even in our death, we will not see the promises of heaven, unless we have believed that Jesus is indeed the risen King. I encourage you to take a step of faith and invite Jesus into your life as your Redeemer by praying something similar to this:

God, I believe You are good, right, holy, and true. Even though I may not understand everything about You or the Bible, I can admit that I know that I am a sinner, who has messed up before and will continue to make mistakes in the future. I am not perfect, but You are always perfect. I am not good enough by my standard, but that is not Your standard. You're not looking for my goodness. You're looking for my love.

I want to love you God. Will you show me how?

Thank You for sending Your Son, Jesus Christ, to die for my sins and make me right with You. I believe that His sacrifice on the cross paid the price for all my sin. Thank You for Your forgiveness. Thank You that I don't have to earn Your love, but that You give it to me as a gift. Please come into my life as my Lord and Savior. I give you my life, my heart, my all. I want to live for You from now on. I surrender my life to You. In Jesus' strong name, Amen.

If you asked Jesus to come into your life as Lord, then it is my deepest joy to welcome to the family of God, sister.

Now it is time for you to live your life as a true disciple of Christ.

God is delighted to be in charge of your life. He never takes us by force, but He will give us His power when we ask for it. Start today, speaking with God as you would a friend, about the areas in your life that are a mess. Ask Him to show you how to live right. Ask Him to show you His purposes for you and how to invest in this world with an eternal perspective. Wait expectantly to see what He'll accomplish in you as you yield every thought and action to Him.

Grab a Bible and start reading the book of John. Ask the Lord to provide a mentor to help you along your brand new journey of becoming the woman God intended. And be sure to seek out a local church that teaches the Word of God as truth. Make an appointment to speak with the pastor and share with him how you've begun a new life as a disciple of Christ.

Scripture References
John 6:44,65; Ephesians 2:8-10; Romans 10:9; Matthew 10:32-33; 1 John 1:9; Acts 2:38; Acts 3:1; 2 Corinthians 5:21-22; Romans 5:1; Romans 4:16; Romans 1:16-17; Romans 10:9-13; Romans 8:5-11; Romans 2:4-5; Romans 6:1-8; Romans 12:1-2; 2 Corinthians 5:17

Leader's Guide

Proverbs 11:25
... those who refresh others will themselves be refreshed.

If I could see you face to face, I would be beaming with a smile, clapping my hands together, and offering you the most sincere encouraging words for even considering leading a small group through this book. I know it is no small task! Likely you are a leader by God's design and He has birthed in you a passion for not only the next generation but a desire to see women equipped with the Word.

Whether you are considering using *Impact Together: Biblical Mentoring Simplified* with your women's ministry team, a group of moms, an online Bible study discussion, or with ETC leaders, may I encourage you to step out in boldness as you seek God's purposes to work through you. However, let me also urge you to seek the covering of prayer and godly counsel. We women can overcommit and end up burnt out, brittle, and bitter. I do not want that for you. But I do want you to receive the blessing that comes from teaching God's Word and imparting His truth for His glory.

Suggested Guidelines

As you consider hosting and leading a small group, keep in mind the following guidelines (which are merely suggestions), will enable you to facilitate a positive experience for yourself as a leader and cultivate healthy relationships within your group.

Prayer

Devote a considerable amount of time to prayer regarding leading a small group before you even make a decision about doing so. Once you have peace to move forward, continue to pray about who to invite to join you in leadership. Throughout the study, dedicate time to praying for each one of the participants. Be sure to open and close each gathering with prayer, seeking the participation of others in this prayer time. Also, find a good friend or an older godly woman to pray for you in your role as leader.

Listen and Learn

The temptation as a leader is to fix a participant's problems. Only Jesus, however, can truly change a life, and He does so through the working of the Holy Spirit. Strive to listen carefully to your participants with a desire to learn about them so you can pray specifically for them. Ask the Holy Spirit to lead and guide your every word, so that when you do respond, you can be confident you are doing so by His grace and for His purpose.

Encourage with Humility

The best thing you can do as a leader is to be in the trenches with the group. Be willing to be vulnerable (with discretion) on areas of struggle and challenge. And at the same time, consider each word you contribute with the filter, "Is this beneficial?" Guard against sharing simply to fill the silence. Let the pause of questions and reflections be a time for God to quicken a person's heart and impart a truth.

Keep It Confidential

From the very beginning, set the policy forth that everything shared within the group remains in the group. I recommend using the expression, "If it is not our story, personally, then it is not our story to tell." I would highly recommend opening or closing each session with this reminder.

Suggested Format

I recommend five weeks dedicated to moving through *Impact Together: Biblical Mentoring Simplified* with a small group. This will allow for a sweet, unhurried introduction session and a meaningful closing fellowship time. I also would suggest an hour and a half for each session. If you feel the momentum of conversation, pause for a moment to let those who must leave part ways, and press on for another fifteen minutes to wrap up. Also, keep the set up and clean up simple. Have a tea basket on hand, coffee, and water, but feel free to pass on something to eat. Most of us don't need it anyhow!

Week 1
Introduction and How to Use
Allow time for each woman to introduce herself, share her faith story and/or mentoring story, and explain why she'd

like to learn more about mentoring.

Week 2
PART ONE:
Myths, Misconceptions, and Pure Motivation
Chapters 1 through 4
Work through Part 1, highlighting different aspects of each chapter and studying the Scripture verses together. Use the Reflection Questions and Impact Challenges for discussion.

Week 3
PART TWO:
Eliminating Excuses
Chapters 5 through 8
Work through Part 2, focusing on the different types of excuses and the Scripture truths. Use the Reflection Questions and Impact Challenges for discussion.

Week 4
PART THREE
The Six Steps of Mentoring
Chapters 9 through 14
Work through Part 3, focusing on the Six Steps of Mentoring. Use the Reflection Questions and Impact Challenges for discussion.

Week 5
PART FOUR
Make an Impact
Chapters 15 through 17
As you move into Part 4, devote time to praying about the opportunities to begin mentoring one-on-one or more formally using the ETC mentoring model. See if any of

the women in your group desire to lead a mentoring group and discuss the process of how this might become a reality. Also make time to study the Scripture verses and discuss the Reflection Questions and Impact Challenges. Spend time in prayer together!

It is truly a blessing and honor to know that God will use this material to impact the lives of the women you are leading and the precious ones that will be influenced by them. As a way of thanking you for leading, you can request a special discount of 10 percent off a life coaching package of your choosing. To learn more about the benefits of life coaching, email me directly at elisa@elisapulliam.com.

How to Form a Mentoring Group

As we've been discussing throughout *Impact Together: Biblical Mentoring Simplified*, the opportunity to mentor can occur in a one-on-one relationship or in a group setting. While the group mentoring idea may be new to you, it is a tested method that provides a beautiful opportunity for impacting lives.

The group mentoring method can be used with tweens, teens, twenty-somethings, or older women. Mentoring groups can be as small as three participants and up to fifteen or twenty. Size doesn't matter. If the Lord grows your group to beyond twenty, you may opt to break into smaller groups. Your gathering can be hosted at a home, school, or church, depending on the setting that works best for you and your participants.

As you consider hosting a mentoring group, you have a choice for what you'd like to call it. ETC, which originally stood for Evening Tea & Chat, has morphed into our Everything (Goes) Tea & Chat, so you can do it at any time of the day! Hosting and leading a mentoring group is simple when you follow these suggestions:

Partnership

Find at least one Christian woman to partner with you in hosting and leading your ministry. A group of two or three is ideal, but not necessary.

Location

Pick a location, such as a home, church, or school, for your gatherings.

Date and Time

Set a bimonthly date with a two-hour commitment.

Invite Girls

Invite Christian and non-Christian tweens, teens, or twenty-somethings from church, your community, or amongst your daughter's friends. Ideally, a group should consider age span, such as ten to thirteen, fourteen to eighteen, nineteen to twenty-two, twenty-three to twenty-six, twenty-six and beyond, moms of tweens, moms of teens, etc.

Tea

Provide lots of hot water and a collection of tea bags or hot chocolate for the girls to grab upon their arrival. Remember, fill your tea basket!

Index Cards

Also have on hand a stack of index cards, pens, and a small basket.

Topic for Discussion

Pick a resource from moretobe.com to download and print out for yourself and the group. Work through the topic in ten to fifteen minutes, teaching the main points. Some of the resources have leader's guides, which will help you unpack the content at a deeper level and implement teaching activities.

Q&A Time

While the topic is being taught, invite your group to write down questions—about anything—on index cards and toss them in a basket. Working with your partner for the next forty minutes, take turns answering their questions with a Scripture reference in the context of life application. Feel free to use a personal example, but remember that less is often more! If you don't know an answer, skip that question with a mention to follow up one-on-one.

Prayer

Close the time in prayer, then encourage the group to get a second cup of tea.

Authentic Relationships

While the group is relaxing and sipping tea, be available for one-on-one conversations. Let the relationships grow naturally.

I hope you'll prayerfully consider beginning a mentoring ministry using our group mentoring format. If you have any questions, please email more@moretobe.com or visit www.moretobe.com for further information and resources.

About More to Be

2 Corinthians 3:16-18 (MSG)
... when God is personally present, a living Spirit ... Nothing between us and God, our faces shining with the brightness of his face. And so we are transfigured much like the Messiah, our lives gradually becoming brighter and more beautiful as God enters our lives and we become like him.

At the heart of *More to Be* is a vision to see women (young and old) become brighter, more beautiful, more like Jesus as a personally relevant God enters their lives through mentoring relationships and resources grounded in biblical truth.

This is what it means to experience life transformed—a life where we answer the call to become more like Him and impact the world around us. With a team of women serving as advisers, contributors, mentor leaders, online group leaders, and life coaches, *More to Be* is fully committed to making biblical truth simple, relevant, and applicable for moms, mentors, and teens.

Through providing simple, easily accessible online resources, *More to Be* is passionate about speaking to the hearts of tween, teen, and twenty-something girls, while also influencing today's moms to be the vessels of truth in their daughters' lives and to see Christian women step out in faith in answering the call to mentor the next generation of young women.

In a culture that promotes being more, the vision of *More to Be* is to see this generation of women and the next enter into a personal relationship with Jesus, so that they may become brighter, more beautiful, more like Him, and go forth to impact this world for His glory!

If you have any questions about *More to Be* or if you would like to invite Elisa to speak at your women's event or youth event for girls, please email more@moretobe.com or visit moretobe.com.

About the Author

Ephesians 3:7
By God's grace and mighty power, I have been given the privilege
of serving him by spreading this Good News.

Elisa Pulliam is a life coach, mentor, speaker, and writer who is passionate about seeing women experience authentic life change through a fresh encounter with God for the sake of impacting the next generation.

In spite of not growing up in a Christian home and spending many years in rebellion, Lisa came to know Jesus Christ as her personal Savior in the fall of 1993. Since then, the Lord has been in the process of transforming her from the outside in and inside out. Because of His extravagant grace, she's determined to help women uncover their God-given purpose and join Him in work as well.

As a speaker, Lisa engages audiences through her transparency, story-telling, good dose of humor, and the practical way she communicates biblical truth. She approaches her messages bathed in prayer, steeped in Scripture, and with the experience of a life coach and coach certification instructor with Life Breakthrough Academy. Lisa seeks to meet women right where they are, while inviting God to bring about the change they crave in every area of life. This is exactly the process you'll find in her book, *Meet the New You: A 21-Day Plan for Embracing Fresh Attitudes and Focused Habits for Real Life Change*, which released in 2015 from Waterbrook Multnomah Publishers.

In addition to leading *More to Be*, she is also on the leadership team of WomenLeadingWomen.us, part of the FaithMomz Network, and a regular contributor to MothersofDaughters.com and TheBetterMom.com.

All of what Lisa does stems from a gratitude for what God has accomplished in her life. She believes each day belongs to the Lord, and seeks to be emotionally present and eternally purposed, especially with her husband of twenty years, Stephen, and their four precious children. Connect with Elisa at moretobe.com and elisapulliam.com.

*If you would like to invite Elisa to speak at your
women's event, mother-daughter event, youth or college-age event
for girls, conference workshop, or retreat on the topic of mentoring
or a message customized for your audience, please feel
free to send an email to elisa@moretobe.com.*

Acknowledgments

1 Corinthians 10:31
...do it all for the glory of God.

My experience as a mentor, and my ability to capture it in this book, would never have been possible without the incredible support of my family. Thank you, Stephen, for being Christ-with-skin-on to me for more than twenty years of marriage and serving as my unofficial life coach. Leah, Abby, Luke, and Kaitlyn, thank you for the ways you've enabled me to invest in lives beyond our family unit and your patience during the many hours devoted toward writing!

I am keenly aware of how our two babysitters demonstrated for me the art of mentoring, which inspired me to want to give this gift to others. Brannon and Natalie, thank you for the way you invested in the lives of our children as you allowed me to serve as your mentor.

I also want to thank the amazing women who serve on the *More to Be* team. They have sustained this ministry for more than five years and I am forever indebted to their partnership.

A special thanks to Sandra Peoples and Kalie Kelch for their editing and proof-reading services.

Of course, anything that comes from my hands is all for the glory of God. Without Jesus, there would be no way I'd be living this life, impacting the next generation, and inspiring you to do the same.

Thank you, Jesus, for this life You've given me and the opportunity to join You in Your work.

Share the Impact

I'd love to hear from you about how this book has impacted your life. Feel free to email me at elisa@elisapulliam.com.

Spread the Word

http://www.moretobe.com

http://www.facebook.com/moretobe

http://www.pinterest.com/elisapulliam

https://twitter.com/elisapulliam

http://www.instagram.com/elisapulliam

http://www.kaleoagency.net

#IMPACT

#impactTOGETHER

Made in the USA
Middletown, DE
17 October 2016